THEME STUDIES
A PRACTICAL GUIDE

This book is dedicated
with loving gratitude to the Lord for giving me the gift
of teaching and to my husband, Lynn, and my children,
Carianne and Levi, for supporting me.

THEME STUDIES
A PRACTICAL GUIDE

HOW TO DEVELOP THEME STUDIES TO FIT YOUR CURRICULUM

SCHOLASTIC
PROFESSIONAL BOOKS

New York • Toronto • London • Auckland • Sydney

Copyright ©1993 by Penny Strube

0-590-49272-1
Designed by Vincent Ceci
Cover illustration by Vincent Ceci
Interior illustration by Drew Hires

Table of Contents

Chapter 1
The Beginning

I will never forget the little boy named Chuck who was in my class the year that I began to use theme study. The day after he received his grade card, he walked up to my desk to announce that I had made a mistake with his social studies grade. Rarely does a child come to you to say his grade is too high! Chuck said, "You gave me a B in social studies, and I didn't do any social studies. I never read the social studies book or did those questions at the bottom of the page." Chuck was referring to the social studies textbook that he had in the year prior to my class. I replied, "Chuck, don't you remember those wonderful ocean and Native American reports that you worked so hard on this quarter?" His astonished reply was, "You mean *that* was social studies?" Chuck had always met with failure when he attempted to read four or five uninteresting, condensed paragraphs of facts about some historical event that he had no prior knowledge of and then answer the required questions that didn't sound at all like the material he had just covered. His frustration was compounded by the repetition of this activity as his class moved quickly through the social studies textbook.

Many teachers are as surprised as Chuck was to discover what theme study actually is. In simple, realistic terms, theme study is in-depth research on a topic (large or small), an issue (current or historical), a person, or an idea in any content area, in which reading and writing are used as tools for learning.

What is Theme Study?

Theme study is defined in a variety of different ways by different people. The diversity in thought is the result of differences in philosophy, educational background, professional growth, and stages of application within the classroom. Each time I enter into a new theme study, I find it new ground to cultivate. Each theme grows into a new dimension because of the fertile bed that was established by the previous themes. Together we are going to explore those dimensions and discover what is involved in a theme study. According to Altwerger and Flores, theme study, which they call *theme cycle*, differs from a theme unit in these distinct ways:

1. A theme unit is teacher-oriented and predetermined. A theme study (cycle) is student oriented, and the topic is negotiated.
2. In a theme unit, the teacher assumes all the responsibility for planning the unit, organizing the activities, and collecting needed materials. Within the theme study, the teacher and all the students share each responsibility connected with the study.

3. Theme units are based on what the teacher chooses as learning goals. The exact opposite is true of the theme study. The goals of the study are based on the prior knowledge of the students and the teacher and the questions generated by the students as they examine the topic.

4. A theme unit uses the theme itself as a tool for learning how to read and how to write. The theme study, on the other hand, uses the reading and writing as tools for learning.

5. The activities are the focus in theme units. With theme study, learning, critical thinking, and problem solving are the focuses. This difference can have a profound impact on your philosophy as an educator and on your students as lifelong learners. (Altwerger, Flores, 1991)

Why Use Theme Study in the Classroom?

I was introduced to theme study at the first Mark Twain Literacy Conference in Hannibal, Missouri. Kittye Copeland, a teacher at Stephen's College Child Study Clinic in Columbia, Missouri, spoke about the type of program that she conducted in her K-6 classroom. As she spoke, a spark of creative energy inspired ideas that I sketched out on my note pad. I began to reorganize my thinking about my classroom. It all seemed like an unobtainable dream, because, unlike Kittye, I was faced with the reality that I taught in a public school. I went to my principal, Elizabeth Boone, and discussed the possibilities of trying Kittye's ideas in my classroom. Not only did Liz encourage me to do it, but she became my mentor. A mentor is someone whose ideas are of great value to you. Liz is just that type of person. She is extremely knowledgeable in the field of education. She had taught for twenty-four years, and after becoming a principal, she continued to take graduate courses and encouraged her faculty to do the same. She inspired and encouraged growth by modeling new strategies of teaching. The moment I received her support, I became truly accountable for the curriculum in my classroom. Liz believed that I could achieve success in this endeavor, and she empowered me with her confidence.

At this point, I had to do some long, hard educational soul searching. I had been asked my philosophy of education at job interviews. As we were advised by our college professors, I had devised a good-sounding philosophy that was all words and held very little meaning to my life as a teacher. My good-sounding, impressive philosophy sentence was no longer useful, because now I was faced with the responsibility of creating my own classroom curriculum. After ten years of teaching, I suddenly needed to read, study, and decide exactly what I believed about how children learn.

My search led me to Dewey, Bruner, Holt, Goodman, Watson, Graves, Altwerger, Flores, Calkins, and many more researchers and theorists. I ferreted out articles in professional magazines and enrolled in classes at the University of Missouri. I had already attained my

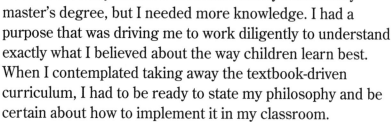

master's degree, but I needed more knowledge. I had a purpose that was driving me to work diligently to understand exactly what I believed about the way children learn best. When I contemplated taking away the textbook-driven curriculum, I had to be ready to state my philosophy and be certain about how to implement it in my classroom.

After spending many hours reading educational theory, considering professional articles, using common sense, and testing theories in the classroom, I had clarified in my mind exactly what I believed about how children learn best. The following six truths became the basis of my new philosophy of education.

1. Children Learn by Doing

This is no surprise. All children learn by doing. (Goodman, 1986) Children learn to read by reading, write by writing, listen by being in tune with the world around them, and speak by sharing what they have learned with others. There is no substitute for being an active learner. Theme centers around the classroom allow the students to touch and become part of the theme. When a child builds a bird house or bakes a pie, the melding of knowledge and creativity easily gives way to success. Even in their failures, they can find success.

2. Children Learn Through the Help of Other Children

I attended a traditional school where sharing thoughts with other children on an assignment was considered cheating. In the business world today, it is obvious that working together is more the norm than the exception. Teams of experts work together to achieve a common goal. Children can do the same kind of sharing to achieve personal and academic success in the classroom. When one child helps another child, there is a merging of two unique perspectives. Because no two people are alike, the two participants bring with them different social skills, language skills, backgrounds, and ways of putting together knowledge. The result is phenomenal! The ideas of both of the children are improved. Children are valuable resources to each other.

3. Children Are Motivated To Learn When They Are Given a Choice

It is amazing how a thing as small as allowing children to make choices can create such a large amount of motivation. Choice is the wheel that moves the sluggish cart of content reading. Choice ignites a child's interest in reading. There is a freedom when children are given a choice and with that powerful freedom of choice comes the responsibility that all freedom carries. Responsibility in turn breeds ownership and ownership gives children's learning a sense of meaning and purpose. When a teacher allows students to make choices about their learning, the experience becomes more thoughtful and richer for the children.

4. Learning Takes Place When There Is a Purpose

The purpose behind any endeavor is the energy source that motivates children to learn. Children (or any of us) learn when they are interested in the subject and their learning is guided by their own sense of purpose. Theme study gives children reasons and purposes to study in the content areas. Learning that takes place when no purpose has been established is easily lost. How many times do we as teachers review all the material that we covered at the beginning of the year in order to help the students remember important facts before a state test? We have to do this, because nonpurposeful learning does not stay with students. True learning takes place when it is used and incorporated into the children's lives. In any given theme study, children will choose that part of the theme that is important and relevant to their lives, and they will establish their own purpose for learning. This is an important step in becoming a lifelong learner.

5. Children Increase Their Knowledge When They Share It

Nothing helps us see connections and clarify ideas better than sharing what we know with others. An audience has a way of helping us listen to ourselves as we expound on the knowledge that we have acquired from reading, writing, and research. The same is true in the classroom when children become experts on particular aspects of their research. Learning is internalizing knowledge to be built upon, compared, generalized, and utilized whenever the need arises. When students present their research to their classmates, they begin to internalize the knowledge they gained during the theme study.

6. Children Are Ultimately Responsible for Their Own Learning

We have for so many years taken away the responsibility of learning from children. Children can be responsible for their own learning. The responsibility of teachers is to teach children HOW TO LEARN. Because children are individuals, they have different learning styles. Individualizing through theme study allows a teacher to become a facilitator and meet the learning needs of each student in the classroom. In return, the students must be responsible for their own personal learning. When we become responsible, for any given reason, we learn more.

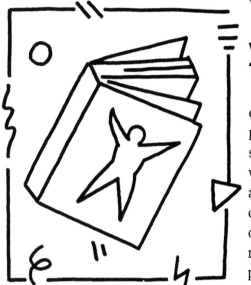

What Are the Educational Benefits of Theme Study?

Never in my life have I jumped into anything new without checking out every aspect of it thoroughly. The teaching profession has appealed to me since I was a small child. The strong professional obligation that I felt toward my students was the force that drove me to examine all the different aspects of theme study. I became a researcher in my own classroom. I began to keep anecdotal records, journals, pieces of written work, individual tapes of recorded readings, and numerous other types of evidence that showed the learning process exhibited by my students. The conclusions that I reached through this small piece of classroom research were overwhelmingly convincing. The implementation of theme study into my classroom curriculum revealed obvious evidence that the students were attaining a higher level of learning. The students found purpose in the material they chose to study, they were motivated to remember and use their acquired knowledge, and they were more interested in learning. This was happening with all my students, regardless of their academic level. The benefits of theme study were surfacing in the areas of motivation and individualization, discovering relationships, and lifelong learning.

Motivation

Motivation is the key to learning. It starts the learning process. Intrinsic motivation rather than extrinsic motivation is desired for the learner, so that children can experience the desire to learn without expecting a tangible reward. (Peterson, 1990) All children possess at least some intrinsic motivation. Curiosity is what sparks learners to begin their search for answers to their questions. Learners are driven by curiosity until they are satisfied by the conclusions they draw from their research. (Bruner, 1966) Learning itself becomes the reward. Another intrinsic motivator is the sense of accomplishment. Learners begin to take pride in their work when they feel ownership of their own accomplishment. Success breeds confidence and that confidence motivates students further, enabling them to take more and greater risks in their reading, writing, listening, and speaking.

Individualization

"There is no unique sequence for all learners, and the optimum in any particular case will depend upon a variety of factors, including past learning, stage development, nature of the material, and individual differences." (*Toward a Theory*, Bruner, 1966) Bruner's quote reminds us why individualizing is so important and why the benefits of individualizing are innumerable. A great number of educational benefits come from being able to take children where they are academically and stretch their learning to match their individual potential. All classrooms are a mixture of low-functioning students, average students, over-achieving students, learning disabled students, and gifted students, coming from various educational and environmental backgrounds. They have individual learning styles, which means they see learning from different directions. The individual attention that a teacher can give to students, regardless of their academic rank in the class, is the most effective tool we have as professionals. Theme study allows the teacher to have individual time with each student. It allows the opportunity to know the child as a student and as a person. Individualizing and personal interest in the children together form a bond that becomes the basis for a good working relationship between teacher and student. The personal touch gives a boost to self-esteem which in turn allows the intrinsic motivators to ensure the flow of creativity within every student.

Discovering Relationships

Once I learned that all knowledge comes from making connections and discovering how all things are linked through relationships, I began to learn, retain, and apply that knowledge by leaps and bounds. Before that enlightenment, all learning was merely a group of fragmented facts that I needed to memorize for a test and were forgotten in a short period of time. No one ever explained to me how to make those learning connections. Theme study not only encourages learners to make connections by linking their new knowledge with their prior experiences, it enhances opportunities to discover those relationships, and models the process.

One particular story stands out in my memory. This story is a prime example of a connection being made out loud. Ryan was a wonderfully athletic student in my room. He would rather hold a football than a pencil any day. The class had decided to study presidents by writing biographies. They began to search the sources available to decide which president they were interested in studying. Ryan was seated over in the resource area of the room looking through

an encyclopedia. He had chosen Volume G in order to read about Ulysses S. Grant. Instead of using the guide words, like any fourth grader, he began to thumb through the volume. All of a sudden, Ryan said, "Mrs. Strube, did you know there was a gold rush in 1849?"

I responded, "Yes, Ryan. What president are you reading about?"

"Don't you get it?" he said. "That's where the Forty-Niners (the football team) got their name."

The excitement of seeing that connection was felt all over the classroom. I stopped what I was doing to grasp that teachable moment with the entire class. Ryan's comment started a discussion in which another student pointed out that the Pittsburgh Steelers got their name from a natural resource in that state and another student mentioned the Oilers.

That one connection stimulated many new connections among the students that had never crossed their minds. The class had identified a new key to understanding the world around them. They had a new perspective on unlocking the mysteries of knowledge through the idea of making connections.

Lifelong Learning

These words, "lifelong learning," sum up my goal as a teacher. I believe that the most important thing I can instill within my students is the idea that learning is exciting, enjoyable, and something they can possess and cherish throughout an entire lifetime. Theme study makes learning synonymous with "exciting", "enjoyable", "interesting", and "lifelong".

Not long after a study of fossils, a humorous event took place in my classroom. Several teachers from an affluent school were coming to observe theme study in my room. We frequently had visitors, so my students felt comfortable with the adults who watched and asked questions. On the morning the visitors were to arrive, I was standing outside my door when the bell rang. I could see a group of adults moving toward my room from the other end of the building. Weaving in and out of the group of adults were two of my students. Nick had a long, large object tucked under his arm, and he was running toward the classroom as if he were racing for a touchdown. As Nick and the visitors approached my door, Nick, somewhat out of breath, announced for all the world to hear that he and Michael had found a dinosaur bone down by his creek. By then the visitors had arrived at my door and were rightfully amused by this inspired student. In my "Please remember we have visitors" voice, I asked the boys to deposit the unknown bone on the observation table and take their seats for the lunch count. You can imagine the excitement Nick caused as he worked his way toward the observation table sharing the bone with other children on the way. As the day progressed, Nick would not be hushed about the bone. He obtained a resource book on skeletons from the library, measured the bone from top to bottom, washed it in the sink, and then in front of the visitors asked if he could get the custodian to help him look into what appeared to be a bullet hole. That was the last straw. I said, "Nick, think about what you just said. Would there be a bullet in a dinosaur bone?" By then, I was so concerned about how my guests must be perceiving this ridiculous display with the bone, that I forgot my prime purpose in the classroom. Nick had gone home, searched for fossils, found a mysterious bone, excitedly rushed it to school, found the tools to examine it, constructed a scientific graph of knowns and unknowns—in short, he had become a lifelong learner because of one theme study that he had been exposed to for three weeks. The visitors had clouded my sense of purpose. Nick was demonstrating exactly what I wanted to see in all of my students. After I came to my senses, the whole class got involved with the mystery. We began to ask questions, collect data, search for information pertaining to bones, and examine the specimen. After much research, Nick finally figured out what the bone was. But the disappointing fact that it was a leg bone of an ordinary cow did not discourage my seekers of knowledge. We had many exciting mysteries to solve after that day.

The benefits that come from theme study revive a teacher and energize that professional to strive for higher levels of learning with every student. Because all humans learn from nature, books, people or other sources, we are in essence all lifelong learners.

Rethinking the Possibilities

Theme study provides children with purposes for learning. The children are encouraged to take responsibility for their own learning. It encourages them to work cooperatively and to collaborate with their peers in a way that promotes a positive sense of community within the classroom. The students begin to develop the ability to think on a higher level. Theme study promotes excitement, and both the students and the teacher become intrinsically motivated. Being able to individualize gives the teacher the opportunity to help the students deal with learning one-on-one. Theme study provides the incentive to discover relationships and make learning connections that can be used for a higher-level learning purpose. Children begin to climb that ladder of potential for which the sky is the only limit!

CHAPTER 2

Thinking About the Study

Another title for this chapter could be a line from the theme song of the movie, *Love Story* : "Where do I begin..." This chapter will explore the many different aspects of planning that take place *before* we engage a theme study within our classroom. Dorothy Watson refers to this strategy as "Planning to Plan." Each of us has a preferred method of sketching out thoughts and ideas. For me, outlines and webs work well to provide a visual picture of topics and related possibilities. In the five years that I have been implementing theme study in my classroom, I have made some amazing discoveries. During the first year, even though I knew in my mind that the students should have choices in every part of the theme, I felt an uncontrollable need to manipulate the theme study by making most of the decisions about the study myself. After completing only a few themes, I no longer felt the need to rule the study. No source could have convinced me as thoroughly as the students in my class that I only needed to facilitate the process. The students competently made choices that not only fulfilled my expectations but went far beyond my most idealistic dreams. The students were exceeding all the requirements that would have been asked of them had I been mapping out the research topics and activities.

Choosing a Topic

When thinking about a topic for a theme study, there are several important factors to consider.

Children's Interest

The topic should be first and foremost a subject that is of interest to the community of learners within your classroom. All the topics chosen for study in my classroom are generated by the interest displayed by the students. It doesn't take long for a teacher to become aware of the interest of the children on any grade level. Children are more than willing to share their interests verbally on a daily basis. The topic of interest may be as ancient and universally liked as dinosaurs, or as current as a world event that is affecting their everyday lives.

Individual Choice

The next consideration is the motivation within the theme. To ensure that the topic will accommodate an in-depth study, I ask myself the following questions:

1. Is the topic broad enough to ensure individual choices about some aspect, so that the whole body of learners will have a desire to study it?

2. Will this topic allow each student to connect with some part of the study in a way that will ensure some degree of success?

3. Will the topic appeal to both genders and all races represented in the class?

Choice is essential! That's really the bottom line. In order to encourage children to be more responsible for their own learning, the teacher/facilitator must be willing to allow the students to make choices about what they learn. Giving children a choice about the curriculum reveals your trust in them as responsible learners. Children need to make choices about their literature, topics for creative writing, and the direction they will take to explore any topic within the theme. Throughout this book, the underlying, most important aspect of theme study is choice. You will hear that word mentioned in every portion of the theme study. In each theme researched in my room, every child has the chance to become an expert on some part of the topic. Over the course of five years, one fact stands out for me as a facilitator of themes: The importance of being the only one in the classroom to study a certain aspect of the topic allows the student to feel ownership within the theme. For example, in a study of oceans, we found at least fifty different forms of sea life for a class of twenty-nine to choose from, so that each child could become an expert on at least one. We listed the fifty different life forms on the chalkboard, and then I proceeded to pull students' names from a bucket. As each individual student's name was picked at random from the bucket, that student selected a sea creature and the choice was recorded on the chalkboard or overhead transparency. No one whose name was drawn after that could make the same choice. In this way, each student was in charge of one piece of the topic that no other student would study. Each child would become an expert. In studies of Native Americans, the children were each responsible for a different tribe located in North America. In the study of endangered animals, the classroom adopted a ring-tailed lemur as a whole-class project, but each individual chose an endangered species to be responsible for throughout the study. I have found the "expert factor" to be one of the best driving forces of motivation connected with theme study. The reason for this will be revealed in a later chapter on Students as Presenters.

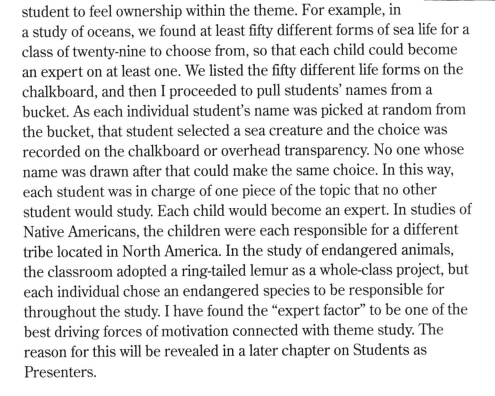

Inventory of Materials

After the topic has been chosen, the facilitator needs to become aware of the materials that are available on that topic. The quality of the study comes from student-generated questions to be explored, but it is virtually impossible to do research if there is only a limited number of resources to support the chosen topic. A facilitator must search and become familiar with all the materials and sources of materials that are available. At this stage of your planning, the quality, number, and availability of resources is crucial. It is essential to have materials that will invite the students to engage in real research. To accommodate an average classroom, a variety and a proper quantity of materials are necessary. In order to assess the different kinds of resources at your disposal, a written inventory can be helpful.

There are different kinds of resources and a variety of means to acquire them. There are three categories of materials available: print materials, non-print materials, and human resources.

Print Materials: There are various types of resources in print. Nonfiction books are usually the most abundant. There is usually a good supply of books on most subjects in the library, either the school library or public library. My students rush to the public library and strip the shelves at the beginning of each theme study. They bring the informational nonfiction books to class and share them with the whole community of learners. There are magazines that complement themes as well. Our school library subscribes to many children's magazines as well as some that would be considered advanced, such as *The National Geographic*. Reference books are another important source of factual information for

THEME STUDY RESOURCE INVENTORY

Print Resources

	Type	Title	Location
1.			
2.			
3.			
4.			
5.			
6.			
7.			
8.			
9.			
10.			
11.			
12.			
13.			
14.			
15.			
16.			
17.			
18.			
19.			
20.			

Non-Print Resources

	Type	Title	Location
1.			
2.			
3.			
4.			
5.			
6.			
7.			
8.			
9.			
10.			

Human Resources

	Trade	Name	Address/Phone
1.			
2.			
3.			
4.			
5.			

students. It is always prudent to offer different sets of encyclopedias in order to accommodate the readers at their own levels.

Nonprint Materials: There are fabulous nonprint items on the market today. Cassette tapes help create the atmosphere and enhance the mood of the theme throughout the classroom. I have purchased cassette tapes of whale songs for the ocean theme study and seasonal music performed on a wooden flute for the Native American study. Videotapes also spark interest in the students. This is a type of familiar and enjoyable means of observing real world happenings. Many of the children in our classrooms will never experience much of what we study, but we can take them to many places with books and videos. My class dove to view the *Titanic* in a small submarine named Alvin and explored the wreck with the help of the remote-controlled underwater robot named Jason Junior, or J. J. We swam in a pond of water and came eye to eye with a crocodile. That certainly isn't an experience I would have in *my* life, but I was able to experience it with the man who had taken that exciting journey in *his* real life. Videos are a valuable source of information. Filmstrips have their place in the fact-finding process. We have an abundance of filmstrips available in our school district. I have found that filmstrips are useful on an individual basis. We have a small projector that can be used by one student or a small group. Each year my students quickly learn to operate the equipment responsibly, and they use the filmstrips at their discretion. They can choose filmstrips that meet their needs in the theme study. Other materials that can be considered as nonprint material are sets of rocks, models of human body parts, scale models of dinosaurs, butterfly nets, binoculars, microscopes, etc. This type of instructional material is an important resource and needs to be on your inventory.

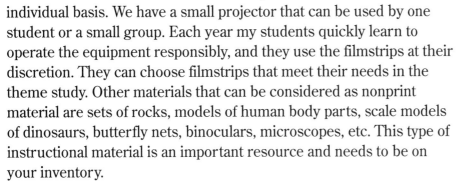

Human Resources: My best sources for locating human resources are my students. They always have a family member or a friend of the family with a profession, trade, or hobby that is related to the study. In many cases, the children themselves are wonderful resources and share a multitude of artifacts with their peers. In previous years, I've been privileged to have Native Americans from a local tribe share rituals, customs, clothing, and jewelry making. We have also been visited by an arrowhead collector, an orthodontist, an author, a poet, a muzzle loader enthusiast, owners of common and exotic animals—the list goes on. The students bond with the human factor. What is observed and learned from books, magazines, cassettes, and videos becomes reality with a human resource.

State Mandates

In our state, as in most states, we have certain state mandates of core competencies and key skills. We are held accountable for teaching these key skills and core competencies by a criterion-referenced test administered to the students in the spring. State mandates are part of the curriculum in the public school setting. I have found that the

mandates are usually so broad that any topic can and does naturally accommodate them. At this stage of planning, a facilitator should be familiar with the mandates required of the students, but it isn't necessary to determine beforehand the specific skills that will be taught during the theme. At the planning stage, being familiar with them and able to identify them is enough.

Children have an uncanny way of surprising us. During the planning for my Native American theme study, I saw the potential for two major core competency key skills to emerge (regions according to climate and natural resources, and land pollution). When I was searching for resources to make available to the students, I ran across a few trade books related to regions and land pollution. I placed these on our resource table along with as many other theme-related books as I could locate. The students previewed the resources for a week before we brainstormed the parameters of our theme study. When I asked the children what they wanted to know about Native Americans, they responded with normal curiosities about their homes, food, clothing, language, etc. Then Jake raised his hand and asked if we could study how the Native Americans used only what they needed, and never made the land dirty. When we were finished brainstorming, the children had decided as a class to study several different aspects of the Native Americans in North America. With the decision to study their homes, the students had incorporated natural resources in every region of North America, and the conservation of those resources led to the study of pollution. The most important lesson I learned was that children make choices that naturally lead to the study of most concepts that mandates set for us.

Strategies

By definition, a strategy is a plan of action applied to attain some goal. Strategies used in a theme study should be applied for the purpose of empowering students to use reading, writing, listening, and speaking as tools for learning. The following is just a sampling of the kinds of strategies that might be utilized as motivators within any chosen topic.

Literature Study Groups

Literature provides one way of understanding the world and making new connections that increase an awareness of the world around us. (Peterson, 1991.) When children read and discuss literature on the same subject as the theme study, it promotes a new dimension to the book and the study. While studying oceans, one literature group chose the book *Call It Courage* by Armstrong Sperry. The dialog among the members of the group turned to the concept of courage. One member brought up the courage exhibited by Mafatu as he fought off a tiger shark in order to save the life of his dog. Another member of the group had chosen to study the tiger shark exclusively as the sea life portion of his ocean report. He shared a complete and accurate description of the tiger shark and its habits. This sort of incident became commonplace, because literature enhances learning. I have found it very beneficial to include a few literature choices that are related to the theme the students are investigating.

Logs

Keeping logs is a useful strategy for the students and the teacher. Logs allow the students to become readers of their own thoughts, as well as opening windows (Harste, Short, Burke, 1988) that allow the teacher to observe how connections are being made and how learning is taking place. There are many kinds of logs. *Reflective logs* reveal what the student has learned and may spark new concerns or questions about the theme. *Learning logs* allow the researchers to give a written explanation of the path they took to discover an aspect of the theme. *Personal logs* furnish a place for personal connections with the theme. The students can begin to see how the new knowledge they acquired is relevant to their lives away from school.

Gathering Information

In order for students to research a topic, they need to be able to apply many strategies of their own. Good readers are readers who use many strategies to comprehend the material they have read. Good writers are writers who have acquired strategies of revision, editing, etc., which enable them to be proficient. Becoming a researcher encourages the students to use the tools of reading and writing to gather information. Helping students acquire the various methods of collecting information may require some strategy lessons to be presented. In your planning stage, you need to be aware of the needs of your students. You may plan to model webbing or mapping with your class, so it can become a strategy they can use on other topics. If you

think the students have a grasp of that strategy, you may wish to model the techniques of using note cards and color coding, outlining, or making a time line. We will discuss these techniques in depth in the chapter on Students as Researchers.

The discussion of these strategies has been very broad, but at the planning stage it will give you an idea of some strategies that will make a big impact on the theme study. As the study begins to develop, it will become apparent that other strategies are needed to enable the students to increase their learning process.

Webbing the Possibilities

The last consideration of our planning is a management aspect. I always make a web or outline of the possible avenues that could be explored. Using a web or an outline allows you to view the possibilities as a whole. Remembering that the students will more than likely be curious about other aspects of the theme, a web of possibilities is usually a good rough draft of the topic, which allows the teacher to be as prepared as possible.

It is also useful to decide on some tentative time goals for the study. These goals may need to be lengthened or shortened depending on the appeal of the topic. I usually try to allow three to four weeks for a theme study in my plans. Some studies have become so intensely interesting and motivating that they have lasted five or six weeks. No two studies are ever alike: the time limits must be flexible. In the chapter on Classroom Management, we will look at ways of making long range and short range plans.

When making plans for a theme study, you should have some expectations of the outcome. There could be some very specific expectations that fit each topic, but the overall expectations are that the students gain confidence, become thinkers and problem solvers, experience intrinsic motivation, and are ultimately empowered to learn.

WEB OF POSSIBILITIES

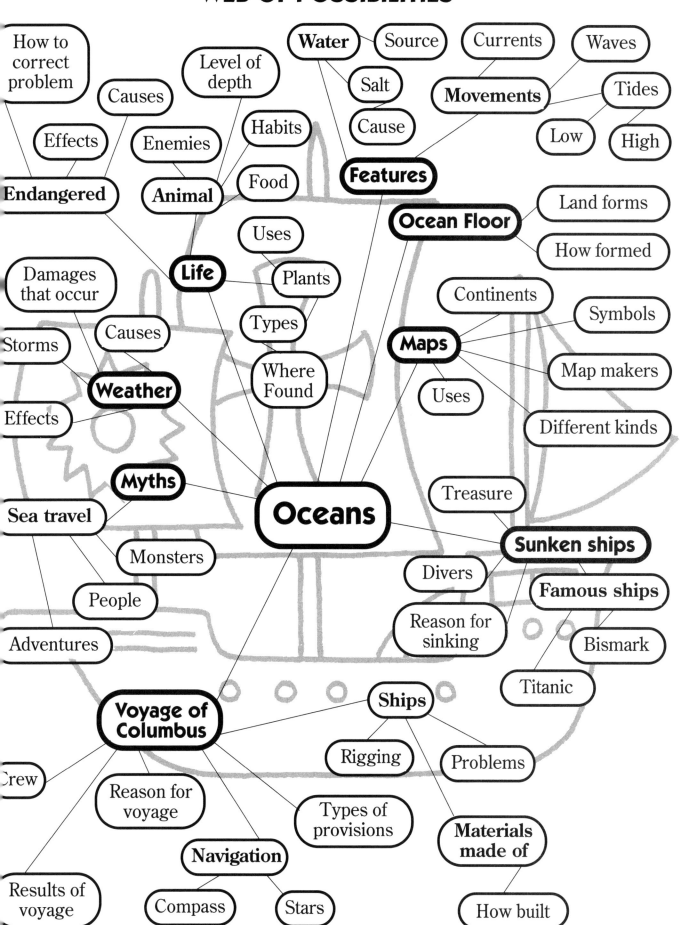

How to correct problem

Causes

Effects

Endangered

Level of depth

Enemies

Habits

Animal

Food

Life

Uses

Plants

Types

Where Found

Damages that occur

Causes

Storms

Weather

Effects

Myths

Sea travel

Monsters

People

Adventures

Oceans

Water — Source

Salt

Cause

Features

Movements — Currents — Waves

Tides

Low — High

Ocean Floor

Land forms

How formed

Maps

Continents

Symbols

Map makers

Uses

Different kinds

Treasure

Sunken ships

Divers

Famous ships

Reason for sinking

Bismark

Titanic

Voyage of Columbus

Ships

Rigging

Problems

Crew

Reason for voyage

Types of provisions

Materials made of

Navigation

Results of voyage

Compass

Stars

How built

Rethinking the Possibilities

You can only be prepared for the possibilities. Students will take a theme study where their interests lead them. You can plan by webbing the possibilities that might occur within the course of the study, but as with all exciting adventures in life, you cannot foresee future events before they happen. Theme study is a learning adventure that the students and the teacher undertake together. The rewards come from entering the situation with an open prepared mind. Teachers can "plan to plan," but they must also be ready to handle the unexpected avenues that the children wish to pursue in their learning process.

CHAPTER 3
Creating a Classroom Environment

Environment is a crucial part of learning. The desire to learn increases when we feel stimulated and comfortable with the surroundings. The classroom can be arranged and decorated to enhance any theme. Room enhancement: **1.** stimulates the students to explore aspects of a theme that they may not have been aware of; **2.** motivates children to ask questions they can research in order to obtain the answers; **3.** provides real purpose for learning; and **4.** allows the children to become part of and bond with the theme. The classroom traditionally is a place where students come to learn. But when the environment matches the theme, the classroom becomes a world where children come to live the learning.

Collecting Informational Materials

With the information collected on our Web of Possibilities and our Resource Inventory, we can begin to collect those resources and have a look at their collective value. The school library and district media centers will provide a vast majority of the materials needed to create an adequate theme environment. Pulling together the nonfiction books, magazines, reference books, films, videotapes, and artifacts allows you to begin with enough materials to pique the children's interest. But this is only the beginning. No matter how many resources you initially offer the class, it is the children who really ferret out the resources that are needed to enhance the meaning of the theme study. A resource display is never complete until the students search the library shelves and their homes. They find resources that relate to aspects of the theme that are of interest to them. The collaborative job of gathering materials can easily continue throughout the entire study. Each time the students are exposed to a library, bookstore, or magazine rack, they will find new information to add to the learning environment.

The collected materials are stationed around the room at appointed resource centers. This provides the learners with consistent places to obtain research information. It has proved efficient to keep different theme categories in several locations, so that students can browse through the resources without keeping others waiting for a turn. This allows more students to utilize the research materials throughout the day. By using several different bookshelves in different locations, the resources for a theme study on oceans could be divided into categories of seashells, whales and other large sea life, small creatures of the sea, storms at sea, ships and sunken ships, ocean fiction, etc. The students enjoy separating the resources into useful categories and displaying them on the shelves.

One year my children chose to study the animals that lived within their home state of Missouri. When they went for their appointed library time, I reminded them that they needed to hunt for any resources that were related to our new theme study topic. When I returned to the library to get them, I was met by an exhausted librarian. The students had located and checked out two rolling carts full of books and magazines. Upon our return to the classroom, I asked the children to begin the process of putting the mountain of books into categories and labeling the groups for easy access. Moments into the task the students realized that not all of the books were relevant. Joe was the first to point out that a book on ostriches would not be needed in our study of Missouri animals. The exotic list began to grow until we had filled up one of the rolling carts with unusable resources. The experience was very educational for the students, because they had to distinguish between the broad theme of animals and the more narrow theme of Missouri animals. The librarian, with good cause, was much less pleased with the educational value of the endeavor. We promised her that in the future we would always discuss the parameters of our studies before we began our resource hunt in the library.

Developing Theme Centers

The use of centers in the classroom gives students the opportunity to get some hands-on, concrete experience with different topics of the theme. The ideas for the centers may grow out of conversations with the children about their interests, innovative activities that have been successful in the past, or resources available to you that support the theme. Children are stimulated by what they see, hear, touch, smell, and taste. Learning centers need to cater to the children's senses in order to motivate their learning. Visual motivation can be accomplished by creating a warm and inviting background around the center. Creating a center near a bulletin board allows you to utilize the background easily. Together the students can make original art for the display or use pre-made materials that the teacher may have as a source of information. There is a vast selection of instructional bulletin boards on the market today. Some ocean packages include diagrams of layers of sea life, food chains, or marine life classifications. Enlarged identification charts of shells, whales, etc.,

make wonderful sources of information for the students to refer to and examine. Either way, the area around a learning center lends itself well to decoration. The decoration should not just exist for the sake of decoration. It should be useful as a source of information to the learners.

The number of centers can vary within each classroom. You must consider the space and materials available. The following are examples of theme centers I have used during an ocean study.

The students in my classroom wanted to study sailors as part of their ocean theme study. Since it was the 500th anniversary of Columbus's journey to America, they decided to study Christopher Columbus. They created two centers that were devoted to Columbus. The Columbus Bulletin Board was a collection of maps and background information on the navigator himself. The children attached a paper holder to the board where they placed any information they had collected about the voyages or Columbus from the newspaper or other sources. It filled up quickly and became a source of current information on the topic. Because Spain had financially supported Christopher Columbus on his voyage across the ocean, the students' interest in the Spanish language increased. This prompted the creation of the Spanish Center.

The Spanish Center contained the English and Spanish versions of several children's books, along with several Spanish/English dictionaries. A tape recorder and headset also provided beginning Spanish lessons. This center became so popular that it inspired several whole-class activities. I began to write Spanish sentences on the daily schedule, to be deciphered at the end of the day. Unknown to me, the

students saved the daily sentences and they used them to make their own personal Spanish word and sentence bank. That collection evolved into their own collection of Spanish sentences in a spiral notebook.

The Whale Center was a center of wonder. There were models of six different species of whales with their babies to touch and observe, along with informational books about each species. On the wall over the display was a poster that included a picture and a description of every known species of whale. A cassette tape of whale sounds was available for listening. The whale songs added a touch of environmental sound to the center. The children could listen and imagine they were diving and swimming with the whales.

The Ship Center contained a vast collection of information on ships of all kinds. The different types of ships were displayed using a book with three-dimensional illustrations. There were non-fiction books on famous ships, sunken ships, and ancient ships. Because of the influence of the books in this center, two other centers were created. The students were so curious about the ship's rigging that they wanted to learn how to tie knots with ropes from a ship. So the Ship Center entered a new phase with long pieces of rope from a sailboat that allowed the children to create all kinds of knots and learn what purpose they served on a ship. The sunken ship aspect opened the realm of diving for treasure. The children were fascinated by the idea of breathing underwater while hunting for treasure. Books on diving were added to the center, along with films about deep sea diving.

The Shell Center began as a simple collection of shells gathered by the students and me. The resource books were different types of guides to identifying shells and species. This center had a more scientific approach to it. The learners could study the shell from several perspectives. They could view the shell with a magnifying glass to observe its structure more closely. They could categorize the collection by size, shape, or type of sea life that had once inhabited it. This center was what I refer to as a living center, because it grew throughout the study. The students kept it alive and interesting on a daily basis by bringing products made of shells to share with the class. They brought lamps, bracelets, purses, pictures, and other items that had been created with shells.

Living nature is the best type of center. A twenty-gallon fish tank in my room allows the students to observe real nature in action. They become mesmerized by the movement of the fish, and

throughout their ocean research, they can relate real, natural occurrences to what they are reading.

These are just a few examples of centers that could be used to create an environment for the ocean theme. Every theme lends itself to centers where the learners can touch, observe, research, and discover throughout the life of the theme study. The students automatically become involved in building centers to fit their interests. The centers never stagnate, but are in a constant state of change as the children bring and leave part of themselves in the centers.

Environmental Tapes

Environmental cassette tapes enhance the classroom atmosphere on the auditory level. It is one thing to read about the ocean and hold models of sea life, but hearing is believing. A tape of the humpback whale singing in the ocean gives a new appreciation to the theme study. Children listen to music and take in all kinds of sounds daily, but when you share the authentic sounds of a topic they are studying, it makes a huge impact on their learning. At the shell center, I placed a book on the coral reef. It had few words, but the students could listen to the sound of a diver swimming in the ocean while they read the book. One student said the sound made him feel like he was the diver in the book. The word spread quickly, and the center was extremely popular. The same feeling could be experienced at the ship center, where the sounds of the ocean breaking on the bow of a ship, seagulls crying overhead, and the crackling of a wooden deck of a seagoing vessel could be heard. Diving and sailing may be experiences that few of my children will ever have in their lifetimes, but with the use of environmental cassette tapes they have the opportunity to add a new dimension to their learning process.

Rethinking the Possibilities

Building an environment in the classroom takes the commitment of both the students and the teacher. Neither can do it alone. Changing the classroom from an ordinary place into a wondrous world of discovery takes the cooperation, creativity, motivation, and desire of the whole community of learners within the classroom. The results are overwhelmingly satisfying. The room itself seems to reach out and encourage the children to become more observant of the world around them and to feel very comfortable with the natural concept of learning.

CHAPTER 4
Inspiring Curiosity

I nspiring curiosity within the learner sounds as if it is a simple task, and with most children it is. The classroom environment should whet the academic appetite of a student, but sometimes it takes something extra. I have found three effective strategies that help boost the natural curiosity inside each and every child.

Incidental Mentioning

This is the strategy that seems to be the most natural for all teachers to implement into their daily classroom lives. Life in a self-contained classroom becomes a community when the members feel comfortable sharing their likes, dislikes, and desires. A teacher is such an influential role model that sharing personal experiences can inspire a real desire to learn.

Two years ago, I became an avid bird watcher. As a result, I felt compelled and eager to share my observations with my students. One morning, I saw an owl sitting on a road sign. I couldn't wait to tell my story at the daily class meeting. It prompted a lengthy discussion of owls, which in turn drew our attention to books we had read about owls. We began to generalize about how owls are symbols for wisdom, how we use plastic owls to scare away unwanted birds, and the conversation continued to build. I'll never forget the warm, autumn day that I saw my first bald eagle. It had flown majestically over my home on Saturday, and I couldn't wait to share my excitement with my classroom community of learners. We discussed so many subjects throughout the year, and my bird experiences would have taken up only a small portion of the collective sharing time. At the end of the year, I told the children that we had enough time for one more theme before summer vacation. I asked them to write down on a piece of paper, in the form of a secret ballot, the one subject in all the world that they personally would like to study. My intent was twofold. I wanted to get a lot of subjects to choose from for the last theme study of the year, and I was hoping to get a personal preference from each child, so that I could conference with them individually and motivate them to conduct their own summer theme study. To my surprise, twenty-eight of the thirty students in my class chose to study birds. I was elated! Through my incidental mentioning of a subject that interested me, I had stimulated their curiosity to the point of desiring the same kind of knowledge. When I tallied the results of the secret ballot, the thought crossed my mind that the children might be choosing birds because I was interested in them, and they wanted to please me. So I began to question their motives for choosing birds as the topic for our last theme study. Joe, one of the students, said, "Mrs. Strube, I want to study birds, because we moved into a new house with a big glass window, and I feed them just outside the window sill." Each answer was different, and none of the students had chosen to study birds in order to please me, which pleased me very much! This is not to say that we as facilitators should implant topics that we want the students to study by dropping constant hints and bits of information. But sharing as a community, the whole class becomes an influence on everyone else, and new fields of learning are opened to all members.

Purposeful Questioning

When children are small, they are constantly asking *why* about every aspect of the world around them. Their natural curiosity is sometimes annoying to an adult with all the answers. However, when the technique is reversed, and "I wonder why…" comes from the teacher, the children are inspired to seek out the answer. Some become obsessed with finding the answer that satisfies them. When a theme study is in the infant stage, the very beginning of its cycle, purposeful questioning is a vital strategy. The desire of any facilitator is for the theme to be one of purpose, quality, and meaningful learning. During this time, before the theme actually begins to take shape, asking questions that invite the learners to search for answers about the theme helps them build questions of their own. Their search for one answer might inspire several other questions that occur as a result of their curiosity. When we were just beginning the Native American study, I asked if anyone could tell us about the *Trail of Tears*. There was no reply. They had no idea what I was talking about, and they requested an explanation. I didn't offer one, but instead I showed them a small book on the subject, invited them to read it, and placed it on the resource table. Curiosity can be inspired and encouraged by thought-provoking questions. This is not as natural as sharing a personal experience, but it can become natural when you get to know your community of learners and understand the directions in which their interests carry them.

Inquiry

Most children don't need any motivating when it comes to being curious. They ask their own questions, find an answer that quenches that question, and then formulate a new question. This process repeats over and over as the learner gains more and more knowledge. As one theme is ending and is in its final week, the new theme environment begins to take shape. That week is a time when the students begin to ask themselves what they want to know about the new theme. On the first day that they begin to investigate the resources available on the new theme, you would think that Willy Wonka had hidden a Golden Ticket inside one of the books. They are like bees

buzzing from one book to another, enriching their minds in many directions. This inquiry generates the curiosity that formulates questions in the minds of the researchers. Their excitement becomes contagious as they begin to share thoughts and observations with the rest of their classmates. This sharing among the learners is what eventually shapes the curriculum of the new theme study. During this beginning time of inquiry, the students and the resources merge to create new thoughts and questions. The learner's curiosity is triggered by being immersed in a variety of resources on a topic. As a facilitator, you just continue to enrich the learner by becoming an active participant in the learning process.

Rethinking the Possibilities

Incidental mentioning, purposeful questioning, and inquiry are simple ways to inspire curiosity in the learner. In essence, the spark that starts when a learner's curiosity is stimulated urges the student to begin the process of learning. Depending upon the individual, the spark of curiosity could become a small campfire or a bonfire that absolutely consumes the learner. The size of fire the spark creates depends upon the individual interests of the learner. Curiosity about the topic seems to be the foundation for building the theme study. This is where questions are born, and the curriculum of the theme study is set in motion.

CHAPTER 5
Brainstorming

Of all the special times encountered in a theme study, I love the brainstorming session the best. It is the time when the theme comes to life. Before this time, the learners have been stimulated by the room environment, engrossed in the resources available, and formulating multi-level questions with prior knowledge and no knowledge. Now it is time for the community of learners to come together and shape the destiny of the theme study. There are many ways to accomplish a brainstorming session. My trusty overhead projector with several transparencies, and grease pencils in several colors, seem to accommodate my needs nicely. Any equipment that allows the whole class to see, read, and participate is appropriate for brainstorming.

Questions

Using a web or list, we begin writing down all the facts that we know about the topic. Everyone in the class participates or is encouraged to participate in this sharing event. Children are eager to share what they know about a subject. It is a matter of pride and satisfaction to be able to contribute to the list being made by the whole class. This can often be a student's first taste of success in the theme study. After we have exhausted all the knowledge we have as a collective body of learners, we then address the question, "What do we want to know?" The students begin to question what is unknown to them. Their questions will reveal just how effective the strategies of incidental mentioning, purposeful questioning, and inquiry into the resources of the classroom were as agents for heightening curiosity. As each question is expressed, it is written down, in no particular order. When the students have no more questions, we look at the total picture of wanted information. At this point, the students try to categorize the questions that are similar in nature. During this whole process of sharing what we are curious about, we speak freely and give our opinions on each of the questions as they are written down. The learners see similarities and begin to draw conclusions about how the questions reveal topics that are alike. They say things like, "I think we could find tools and weapons in the same books, because they are made in the same way from the same materials. Let's put those two things together as one question." Later in the Native American study, they included the question about dancing with questions about games and celebrations. As the teacher, I am also part of the community and have the privilege of asking questions that can be added to the list. After you have completed several theme studies, you will realize, as I did, that children ask the same questions that you think are necessary to create a quality study. When you realize that the body of learners, whose academic growth is your responsibility, is asking the very questions that you deem relevant and important to the study, then the burden of mandates is lifted from your shoulders and the urge to control the curriculum vanishes.

When the "What We Want to Know" part of the brainstorming session is completed, the students turn their questions into topics to investigate in order to find the answers. This is an example of how one class turned their questions into topics for research.

What We Want to Know

1. Transportation (How did they move from place to place?)
2. Chiefs and Warriors (Who were some famous Native Americans?)
3. Food (What kind of food was available in each region?)
4. Games and Celebrations (What kind of recreation did they enjoy?)
5. Language (How did the different tribes communicate?)
6. Homes (What did their homes look like and what were they made of?)
7. Clothes (What kind of clothes did they wear and how were they made?)
8. Illnesses (How did they heal the sick people?)
9. Region (Where was the tribe located and what natural resources were there?)
10. Education (How did they get an education and what did they learn?)
11. Weapons and Tools (How did they make their weapons and tools?)
12. Crafts (What kinds of things did they make—pottery, rugs, necklaces, etc.?)
13. Tribal Rules or Laws (How and why were the rules made?)

This is a complete and comprehensive list of what the learners were truly interested in knowing about Native Americans. This is not to say that when they were engaged in researching the answers to their questions and came across a topic not included that they ignored it. Quite the contrary. The list of questions and topics grew throughout the study. Those individual additions to the research added an element of excitement as the study progressed. This increased the desire to search continually for new ideas and greatly decreased the possibility of boredom setting in because the study was limited to just what was agreed upon.

Expert's Choice

In Chapter 2, the importance of becoming an expert on some aspect of the theme was described as a "driving force of motivation." Students make personal choices during the whole-group brainstorming session. Since each child will be responsible to the body of learners for the information collected and presented, it might be necessary to break into some individual brainstorming time to research and think about the choices. The students once again return to a state of inquiry. They return to the available books and resources with a more specific task in mind. Instead of just getting familiar enough to ask questions, as they did to prepare for the whole-class brainstorming session, they now need to do a more detailed search to find their individual area of interest within the broader topic. The students usually feel comfortable looking at lists of ideas about the theme. With Native Americans, the list might come from a map of all the tribes that live in North America. With oceans, a picture or list of life under the sea might serve as a guide for choice. Charts of organs for each of the body systems, globes with pictures of endangered animals, time lines of inventions, historical events, etc., all produce a visual listing for the students to use when making choices.

While the students are concentrating on their individual selections, the teacher facilitates by moving from one student to another, making sure that each student is successful in finding the material needed to make an informed decision. At the same time, the teacher can be compiling a list of possible choices on a transparency as a visual aid.

There are many ways to accommodate the children with their choices. The ideal is to be sure that all students get their first choice. However with a class of twenty or thirty, there will very likely be an overlap in choices. This is not to say that two children couldn't be co-experts and study the same thing, but from my experience, children achieve the greatest sense of success when they own a piece of the research all by themselves. In any given topic, there are so many possible choices that the abundance allows each student to be satisfied.

One way to ensure children's choices is to have a "first come, first served" policy. The children make their choices and report their choices to the teacher, who records each request. If a later choice duplicates a previous choice, the teacher helps that student to search for a new choice. The individual attention from the facilitator seems to diminish the disappointment. In most cases, students like the new choice more than the original.

Another way to accommodate choice is to create a large list prior to the brainstorming session and display it for all the students to see. As a student's name is pulled at random from a jar, that child names a preferred choice. As each choice is made, the child's name is written beside the choice. The list needs to be large enough to keep from trapping a student into having to choose from six or seven last resort items. The students always need to feel that their choices reflect *their* interests and are not just leftovers. Many times, if the last choices do not satisfy the desires of the students at the end of the draw, they decide to do more research and report their choices at a later time.

The choice for the expert part of the theme has such a great impact that it should be done with a great deal of thought. If the students really cannot find a part of the theme that will satisfy their interests, the choice can easily be made as the in-depth research is being conducted on the theme. Likewise, a choice can be changed. If the students find something of more interest while they are gathering information, they should be allowed to make the switch. Few switches will ever be made, but the assurance that they are not locked into one choice eases the stress of making the perfect choice at the beginning.

Choosing Activities

The next question to be considered in the brainstorming session is "What activities do we want to incorporate in the theme study?" Children are so creative. When it comes to deciding on activities that are appropriate for the theme and help achieve the chosen goals, the children are the inventors. There are no better ideas about activities than those found in the minds of the children. Activities of all types serve to enhance and move the study from beginning to end. The first year I used theme study, someone gave me a list of projects that had been printed in a professional journal. I tucked it away for brainstorming days, so that I would have a pocketful of ideas for the students to choose from. That was probably one of the most useless pieces of paper that I ever collected. The children always think of fantastic projects and activities that embellish the theme study.

For instance, during a study of the human body systems, a student came up with the idea of making models. Each of the students would be responsible for their chosen body organ or part. The results were phenomenal! One student created two sets of teeth. She bit into some school-issue gray clay, mixed plaster, and poured it into the impression. The final product was a perfect replica of her own teeth. Other models included a working heart that pumped red water, lungs created by

using sponges, and a jar of acid used to demonstrate how the stomach breaks down food. The idea of creating models turned out to be an outstanding theme activity.

The suggested project ideas are written down for the whole class to view. Since the field of ideas needs to be narrowed down, the process of give and take begins. Some of the ideas are joined together to make one, some are completely a new creation built from several other ideas, and some are accepted just as they were submitted. Through this collaboration, individual, small-group, and whole-class activities can be designed. The activities might include art projects, crafts, special days to celebrate the theme, re-creating events through drama, writing books, expressing concerns, requesting information through letter writing, or cooking. The activities will be as diverse as the interests and talents of the students in your classroom.

Gathering Information

There are many different ways for children to gather and record the information they acquire. By the end of the year, after many theme studies, most children feel comfortable with a variety of methods. The students, as a class, vote on a new method for each report. The method is used by the whole class to gather information for the study. They might choose to make a web, use note cards, create a time line, develop an outline, keep a log, or design a flow chart. Changing the method of collecting information for each theme allows the researchers to discover which method best meets their individual needs.

After deciding the manner in which the information will be collected, the next consideration is how much information to collect. Usually there is one child who wants to take twenty notes, and one who wants to take a hundred. We compromise somewhere in between. One year the class decided to use minimum requirements, so they would have a common goal, but those who wanted to take more notes could do so freely. On the last study of the year, I encourage students to think back on all the information-gathering techniques that were used during our theme studies. The students, individually, not as a whole class, choose the method of collection that best suits their personal needs and styles. They also make choices on the number of notes they intend to collect. They weigh the choices thoughtfully, and as a class they choose a variety of research methods. This encourages independent out-of-school theme study by showing the students that real research is done by using methods that work best for them.

Planning for the Contents of the Final Product

Planning for the final product is an essential part of the theme study. It allows the students a view into the future, so they can plan on how to bring a theme to closure. Along the way, with a majority of class consensus, the plan can always be revised. But during the whole class brainstorming, some plan for the contents of the final product needs to be made. A final product can take several forms. Because there is a rich variety of ideas in the minds of the students, the following are just a few ways in which new knowledge about a theme can be presented.

Report

Writing a report is a comprehensive way to record and present the knowledge accumulated by the learners. The report that the students produce as their final product has many facets that need to be addressed during the brainstorming session. The question of what we wish to have included in the final product comes from the knowledge of what real reports or books include within their pages. A few components that the students may wish to include are a cover (individual art creation, or whole-class creation printed for everyone), title page, table of contents, illustrations, diagrams, and bibliography. Each suggestion submitted to the class is revised or enhanced and then voted on for approval. The final draft of the report can be bound in book fashion by inserting a spiral, stapling, sewing with thread, punching holes and binding with paper fasteners, or gluing the pages in a hard cover. Any of these methods makes the report appealing and usable for students' future reference. The pride of authoring a report and seeing and feeling the tangible final product increases the desire within the learners to research a new topic.

Mobiles

Mobiles, made with a dowel rod or a hanger, can become an interesting and innovative means of displaying learned knowledge. Broad themes, such as explorers, can best be served and presented by having each student concentrate on one explorer. Then as a whole class, they could present their explorers in historic order, as they would appear on the time line. The mobile could include a title strip, an informational facts strip, a diagram or map of the explorer's journey, an analysis of the impact the discovery had on the world then and now, a drawn portrait of the explorer, and a bibliography strip. The amount of information and the display design would be decided as a whole group.

Newspaper or Magazine

A newspaper or magazine is an innovative way to present gathered knowledge on any theme. Not only do the students learn about the theme, but they also become knowledgeable about the format and function of a newspaper or magazine. This familiarity is necessary before they can make decisions about the contents of their joint final product. There are many other reasons why this type of format is profitable to each student. It allows and encourages social interaction between the students within the classroom. It creates an atmosphere that promotes responsibility on the part of each student to contribute to the good of the whole body of learners. It increases the students' awareness of the interactions that must take place in order to create a quality final product that will bring pride to the entire class. Because of their hands-on experience, the students begin to see how a daily newspaper or a monthly magazine works in the real world. When the theme is completed, the students might decide to keep the classroom newspaper or magazine in circulation for the rest of the school year. It could be utilized as a means of informing parents of classroom and school events. A monthly classroom project like this opens communication between home and school.

Setting Goals

After the theme has been thoroughly mapped out in every area, time limits and due dates for each goal must be decided upon. When working in a time frame of three to four weeks per theme, it is very important to establish responsible deadlines. In my classroom, I create a computerized calender containing graphics that match the current theme. As a whole class, we negotiate specific due dates for the contents of the final product and plan dates for theme activities to be held. After a date is agreed upon, it is recorded and each learner is held responsible for the work involved in meeting that goal. Since the children have a big part in negotiating the due dates, they take the responsibility very seriously. Along with the privilege of choice comes the awesome responsibility of meeting the common goals.

Children's Choices

The greatest motivating factor when creating a theme study is the fact that the children have a choice in every aspect of the study. The learners choose what they want to know about the topic, what activities they would like to participate in, what methods of gathering information they will use, the nature and contents of the finished product, and they determine the time limits for accomplishing their goals. Every part of the theme has been established through the democratic procedure of making choices. This is the key to unlocking the natural learner in every child. Despite the academic standing of each student, choice gives the incentive for all students to reach their potential. This is a major contributing factor to the success of theme study. All students are driven by the desire to choose what they feel is relevant to their life in and out of school.

OCEANS

THINGS WE WANT TO KNOW ABOUT:

1. Movement—waves, tides, currents
2. Description—how many, how deep, size, location, type of water
3. Sailors—Vikings, Columbus
4. Maps—different kinds, map makers, symbols, continents
5. Sea Life—food, enemies, level they live on, habits, how they move, protection
6. Pollution—causes, effects
7. Storms—kinds, how formed, damage they cause
8. Sunken ships—famous, treasure, divers, reasons for sinking

THINGS I WILL PUT IN MY REPORT

1. Title page
2. Table of contents
3. Maps—oceans, continents, explorers' routes, ancient maps
4. Illustrations—ships, people, treasure, sea life
5. Cover

HOW I WILL DO MY REPORT

1. Use 3 sources—encyclopedia, magazine, trade book
2. Make a web of my notes
3. Write sentences for each bubble of my web
4. Put my sentences in paragraphs (ROUGH DRAFT)
5. Conference with my teacher
6. Write my final draft

Rethinking the Possibilities

The brainstorming process is a vitally important part of the theme study. The whole theme begins to take shape, and the students become excited and motivated as they embark upon a new study.

Throughout this process, the underlying currents of choice and democratic decision-making motivate and instill responsibility in the learner.

Without the concept of children's choices, there would be no theme study as we know it. It would become a dictatorial, teacher-driven, teacher-motivated study, and the responsibility and accountability for learning would be placed squarely on the teacher's shoulders. Giving children the opportunity to make choices creates a totally different atmosphere—one that encourages learning to take place.

The whole brainstorming session could be compared to a potter just beginning a new piece of pottery. The theme is chosen and placed on the brainstorming wheel to be shaped. The students' questions begin to shape the theme into a unique piece of pottery. The chosen activities spice up the theme to keep the interest high among the learners. Having the choice of how the final product will appear holds the children responsible throughout the creation and the completion of the theme.

CHAPTER 6
Students as Researchers

The stage is set. Everything needed to engage in a meaningful and purposeful theme study is ready to be set in motion. The students are so motivated by their choices, that as the teacher you have very little to do with the theme's launch. On the opening day of research, the excitement runs high. By this time, the children need no introduction to the books, no overview of the theme, or anything else. They just want to begin their research! The process of research doesn't follow specific stages, but there are certain procedures that progress naturally as the learner reads and acquires information.

The researchers need to be absorbed in their reading, but at the same time it is necessary to record their findings in some manner. The students can collect information by using one of two types of methods. The information can be placed into random categories to be sorted later, or it can be sorted as it is obtained and placed into precategorized locations. With the precategorized method, students can collect information on a web, outline, or time line. If the students want to use the method of random categories, they can record their information on index cards or in the form of a log/journal.

The method of collection is chosen and agreed upon by the whole body of learners during the brainstorming session. With each theme, the students choose a new way of collecting notes, and they all use that technique during the existing theme study. This allows the students to have a choice in deciding a new method for each theme. The variety provides the opportunity for all students to discover the information-collecting technique that accommodates their style of learning.

Any form of information collecting/note taking requires knowing how to research and record information. There are many factors to be considered before the pencil is put to paper. Each technique and strategy should be modeled for the whole class as the need arises and the researchers progress through the theme.

Key Words

Since reading in the content area is more difficult than reading fiction, it is important to explain to the students how to get the most from their reading. A good place to start is with key words. Explaining to students that they are not allowed to copy straight from the book comes as a surprise to some. But after hearing the explanation of plagiarism, the students never question it again. They understand the concept of ownership from their own creative writing. They are very protective of their thoughts and ideas and can understand why adult authors would feel the same way.

In the key word modeling session, the students are asked to pick any resource available and find a paragraph that interests them. Student participation is extremely important to the learning process. I ask for volunteers to read aloud the paragraphs they have chosen. As each volunteer reads to the class, the listeners jot down what they think are important facts in the paragraph. The paragraph may need to be read a second time for the listeners to grasp the complete idea of the subject. The students take turns sharing what they feel are meaningful sentences in the paragraph. Focusing on individual sentences narrows the field of words.

The next question is, "What are the key words in the sentence that will be useful to me in my research?" This is the tricky part. Students must decide how many words are too few, how many words are too many, and how many words are just right. This could be different for each student. The number depends on how many words it takes to help the children remember the information that they read when it is time to synthesize their findings. They do not want to select so few words that the meaning of the information is lost, and they do not want to write so many that only a few articles and conjunctions are needed to re-create the sentence in its original form. The solution is to select enough key words to retain the knowledge, but few enough to encourage writing original sentences of their own.

For example, in the sentence that follows there are many different ways a child studying peregrine falcons could transform the new information into key words.

"A peregrine falcon reaches the speed of almost 200 miles per hour when it dives to attack its prey."

Sample A

1. Peregrine falcon reaches speed almost 200 mph diving attack prey

Sample A exhibits the method that beginning researchers usually take because they are afraid they will forget the information when they need it. Few words were omitted from the sentence, which makes it almost impossible for the researchers to restate the information in their own words.

Sample B
1. speed 200 prey

This sometimes happens when the student researchers are anxious to show how much they can remember. Unfortunately for them, it is usually the case that they do forget and have to spend more time relocating the information before they can use it. It is true that if they are able to remember the information this well, they are truly internalizing the new information almost immediately. Very few children are at that advanced stage in the elementary and intermediate grades, and the meaning of the information is almost always lost. One of two things can be done. The student can either return to the original source and relocate the information, or they can forget the information altogether.

Sample C
1. reaches speed 200 mph diving at prey

This sample shows the student has learned to recognize the important words that carry meaning in the sentence. The key words may be words that they know look important but whose meaning they are unsure of. Encouraging the students to use the dictionary to discover the meaning of the unknown word and to write the definition in their own words increases the students' vocabularies and teaches them about synonyms at the same time. If a student did not know what the word *prey* meant in Sample C, the word *game* could be substituted as a key word. Key words are only valuable if they reflect the knowledge of the researcher.

After the whole-class modeling session is completed, it is helpful to have the students break into small groups to continue the practice with key words. They should share their chosen paragraphs and discuss them with their peers. This will reinforce their understanding of key words and encourage their participation in the learning community. They will help each other throughout their research.

Taking Notes

After the students have a grasp of what key words are and the function they play in effective note taking, they can begin to collect information in a usable form. Being an effective note taker is a necessary part of being a good researcher. Notes are visual pieces of thought. They become our way of thinking on paper. Most ideas become very clear when we see them in writing. Notes are a way for students to communicate with themselves. Modeling note taking techniques and strategies as a whole-class activity at the beginning of each theme helps to build a stronger understanding of the process within the students.

Recording information can be accomplished in many ways, but four of the most commonly used methods demonstrate the variety of different techniques that can be used. Webbing, outlining, index cards, and discovery logs involve different modes or styles of collecting information.

1. Webbing

Recording notes in the form of a web seems to be the easiest way to organize information. Each piece of the web is a category to be described or a question to be answered. When the student researchers find a fact or idea that they consider valuable, they write the key words on the web, branching out from the category to which it is related. In the example below, the subject or theme is written in the middle. The categories of interest to the student branch out from the center. From that point each piece of information is connected to its appropriate category.

2. Outlines

An outline can be used as a tool for recording information, too. This takes more concentration and thought about where to record the information, but when the notes are collected, they are well organized. Each Roman numeral might represent a question to be answered. The rough draft outline form provides unlimited space to record information collected, but it takes a little effort to decide where on the outline the information most appropriately belongs. Because of the uncertainty about how many pieces of information will be found for each Roman numeral, the students generally create a large empty outline form to accommodate their findings. At the end of the research, the outline will look like a typical rough draft. Some sections will need to be expanded to accommodate the large quantity of information found, while other sections will need to be reduced in size because less information was

---

ENDANGERED ANIMALS

(Giant Panda)

I. What does a panda look like?
  A. Body
       1. White with black legs
       2. Black patches around eyes
  B. Weight
       1. Up to 350 pounds
       2.
  C. Paws
       1. Pads like flesh
       2. Have "extra thumb"
II. What do they eat?
  A. Bamboo shoots
       1. Main food
       2.
  B. Plants
       1.
       2.
  C. Fish and small rodents
       1.
       2.
III. Where do they live?
  A. Bamboo forests
       1. Upper mountain slopes
       2. Western, southwestern China
  B.
       1.
       2.
  C.
       1.
       2.

WEB

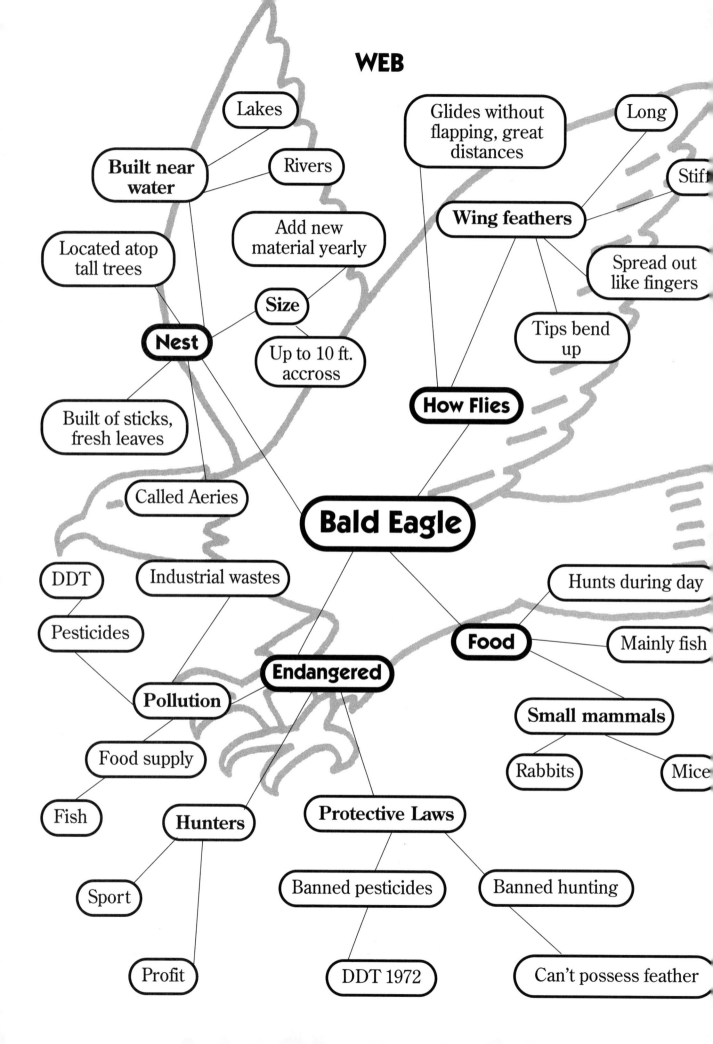

Bald Eagle

Nest
- Built near water
  - Lakes
  - Rivers
- Located atop tall trees
- Add new material yearly
- Size
  - Up to 10 ft. accross
- Built of sticks, fresh leaves
- Called Aeries

How Flies
- Glides without flapping, great distances
- Wing feathers
  - Long
  - Stiff
  - Spread out like fingers
  - Tips bend up

Food
- Hunts during day
- Mainly fish
- Small mammals
  - Rabbits
  - Mice

Endangered
- Pollution
  - DDT
  - Pesticides
  - Industrial wastes
  - Food supply
    - Fish
- Hunters
  - Sport
  - Profit
- Protective Laws
  - Banned pesticides
    - DDT 1972
  - Banned hunting
    - Can't possess feather

discovered than the researcher anticipated. Because of the uncertainty about the amount of information that will be uncovered, it is impossible to know ahead of time what the final form of the outline will look like.

The example on page 53 illustrates what a rough draft outline might look like after the information from just one resource was entered.

This was by far the most difficult way to record information for children, but they enjoyed the challenge it provided as they developed their research skills.

3. Index Cards

For bigger, more extensive research, note cards provide an alternative method of note taking. By using 3" x 5" or 4" x 6" index cards, the researchers are free to record facts or ideas from many categories as they find them. They do not have to worry about where to place the information at this time, as they do on a web or an outline. They just read, select, and record. In this way, the in-depth research is not interrupted, which allows the researcher to move freely from question to answer to new question without stopping to categorize each new piece of information. The key words are recorded to form notes on a card and numbered according to the order in which they are found. No number is ever duplicated, so the researcher can keep track of the cumulative amount of notes recorded.

In the example that follows, the theme of endangered species is being investigated. The researcher's expert report is on the giant panda. As the researcher reads about pandas, the list of questions developed during the brainstorming session is there alongside the index cards. The students are reminded of the areas of interest that they wish to pursue, but they do not worry about the order in which a note is recorded. With the unanswered questions in their minds, this is a time of pure research, when they can read, discover, and record their findings. This is a sample of what the researcher might record on the index card.

You can see how the notes do not follow a central topic or category. They are just random pieces of information pertaining to several different categories. Index cards can be

GIANT PANDAS

1. Live in central China

2. Look like teddy bears

3. Only small number left

4. Live in high mountains

5. Live in bamboo forest

6. Threatened by poachers

7. Raccoon family

8. Don't hibernate

9. Eat 40 lb. bamboo stems daily

10. Losing habitat

used for a second purpose at the same time. The color of the index card can indicate what kind of resource was used. For example, encyclopedias could be recorded on yellow cards, nonfiction books on blue, magazines on green, films on pink, etc. If the student records the title, author, volume number, publisher, date of publication, or whatever is appropriate for the type of resource, at the top of each card, then the source of each note recorded can be easily relocated if the researcher should need to refer back for clarification. This will help clarify the meaning of any key words that make up the recorded notes, as the students move on with the meaning-making process.

4. Discovery Logs

Using a discovery log, or any kind of log, is a professional way of recording information or data. By using an instrument that real scientists use, we encourage authentic actions on the part of the student researchers. Constructing a discovery log is quite simple. The students create their own by sandwiching a large chunk of notebook paper between two pieces of art or drawing paper. They staple the booklet along the spine and personalize it to their own specifications. There is such a diversity in how a discovery log is arranged that it would be impossible to list suggestions, however, many consistent features emerge from log to log. Most have a creative title that announces the subject of the study. Just inside the front page, most student researchers establish a table of contents to aid them in locating the recorded information more quickly. Each page of the log usually

has a distinctly different function, which is designated by a heading written at the top. The questions from the brainstorming session are transferred into the log and plenty of empty space is left to record the answers. Many times the answer to one question generates another question, so the students leave plenty of blank space under each question. Charts, diagrams, graphs, and other illustrated information are usually recorded in the pages of a discovery log. Recording notes in this particular form allows the students to keep all of their research together in one place.

These are just a few of the ways for collecting information in note form that I have found to be productive with children. No matter which technique the students use, the end result will give them a firm foundation from which the final product will be molded.

Creating Sentences

After the student researchers have exhausted the resources, found the answers to their questions, and recorded all their valuable notes, it is time to put the knowledge they have gathered, using webs, outlines, index cards, or discovery logs into their own words. In this part of the process, the learners get to express the knowledge they have accumulated and assimilated in their own words and their own voice. This is a significant time for your students, and probably the hardest part of the process for them to grasp. They must become aware that the notes they have collected are the foundation of their research. According to Graves, voice is the implant of ourselves on our writing (1983). When the students are absorbing the notes that they have recorded, considering the meaning the notes hold, and beginning to comprehend the impact of new knowledge, their voice will emerge in the writing of their very own original sentences. As teachers, we can spot right away those students that are experiencing the full benefits of their research and those who are struggling to move from how the books expressed ideas to how they want to express ideas. My favorite reply to unoriginal sentences copied by the students is, "That sounds booky. Let's make it sound like you." We need to encourage children to develop their own voice in writing. Many children are afraid to allow their voice to be heard in their work. They think teachers want to hear the more professional book voice rather than their collection of simple thoughts. It is easy to say, "Turn the key words into your own words and make a sentence that comes from your mind. Don't make yourself sound like the book you took the notes from. Just write it the way you would say it." But in the student's reality, that is easier said than done.

Here are two examples derived from the same key words. The original sentence from a resource might read:
"The Milky Way Galaxy in all of its expanse contains billions of stars."

The key words that a child might choose are: Milky Way Galaxy expanse contains billions stars

The child who is struggling to find his or her own voice might write the following sentence:
"The Milky Way Galaxy in expanse contains billions of stars."
As you can see only a few words from the initial sentence were omitted. The sentence sounds so much like the book that on the surface it appears to have been copied.

Even though the key words were similar to the sentence so the researcher would not forget the meaning of the note, children who are comfortable with their own voice would write something similar to the following: "The Milky Way Galaxy is so big that it has billions of stars in it."

Helping children find their voices cannot be done in a group setting. This delicate matter takes a personal touch. Having individual conferences with all students encourages them personally, stimulates their creative ideas, empowers them to produce quality work, and builds the confidence they need to write in their own voices. Once the students begin to feel comfortable with their own writing voices, creating sentences will become an easy task for them to accomplish.

Sorting Information

After the sentences have been completed, the next step is to analyze the accumulated information. In the case of webbing or outlining, the categories are already established by either the headings in the bubbles of the web or the Roman numerals of the outline. With these methods, the procedure of sorting the information is already accomplished.

All the students need to do, after using one of the precategorized techniques, is turn each set of key words into an original sentence.

However when index cards or discovery logs/journals are used, sorting or categorizing is needed. One method of categorizing information, which we call color coding, has been very successful in my classroom. Color coding is a simple way to visualize categories by color. By using crayons, colored pencils, or markers, a different color is assigned to each of the topics that were chosen during the brainstorming session.

Below is a partial list from the brainstorming session of a Native American theme study. This list fragment represents a few of the topics that the students wanted to learn about when they conducted their research.

(red)	**1.** Transportation
(blue)	**2.** Food
(green)	**3.** Games and Celebrations
(yellow)	**4.** Languages
(gray)	**5.** Homes
(orange)	**6.** Clothes

Where I have placed the color word, the children would have made a simple mark, slash, or dot of the color. In order to remember the colors and the topics, the students either carry around their brainstorming list or copy the topics on another index card and put a colored mark by each one, thus creating a portable color key.

The topics become categories in which the researchers can group their sentences. Each sentence is reread, classified by category, and a color is placed by it.

14. The Haida tribe placed totem poles in front of their homes to display their family emblems.

For sample sentence 14, the student researcher would make a gray mark in front of its number. This identifies it as part of the group of sentences relating to the topic of Homes.

Analyzing each sentence in this manner impels the student researchers to discover three things about their research. First, as the researcher rereads the sentences, it reviews the content of each one in the student's mind. Second, it reinforces the decision-making process concerning which sentences support what specific topic. And third, the researcher can assess which topics have only a few sentences supporting them and will require extra research to explain the concept adequately.

Arranging Information

After all the sentences have been sorted into categories, the children turn their thoughts to creating paragraphs. As is true in all paragraphs, there is a need for a unity of ideas to be expressed. The sentences need to support the main idea of the paragraph in a way that conveys to the reader exactly what the researcher wants to share from the results of the research.

In the cases of webs, outlines, and other precategorizing techniques, the researcher's original sentences are already grouped together by topic, but most of the time they lack a sense of arrangement. Usually a main idea sentence needs to be created, and the supporting sentences need to be arranged into a well-organized paragraph.

When using the color-coded sentences, a variety of strategies can be implemented to accomplish the goal of creating meaningful

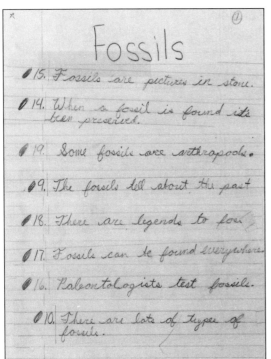

Fossils

15. Fossils are pictures in stone.

14. When a fossil is found its been preserved.

19. Some fossils are arthropods.

9. The fossils tell about the past

18. There are legends to fos

17. Fossils can be found everywhere.

16. Paleontologists test fossils.

10. There are lots of types of fossils.

paragraphs. The students can create paragraphs by cutting apart all the sentences, putting them in stacks by color, arranging each stack of sentences in an order that creates the most effective paragraph, and gluing the pieces on another sheet of paper. This creates an opportunity to manipulate the sentences, organizing and reorganizing them until the students are satisfied with the order and structure of their paragraphs.

Shortly after I began using theme study in my classroom, a memorable event took place that still brings a chuckle in the teacher's lounge whenever it is recalled. It was early in September, during the first theme study of the new school year. The whole class was ready to make paragraphs and was waiting for my promised modeling session to begin. We were going to work together and learn together. I had asked the students to leave an empty line between each sentence and not to write on the backs of their papers. All the students had followed those directions, and we were ready to proceed. The color coding had been accomplished, and there were sentences of various colors on each of the pages. In order to put all of the same colors together, it was necessary to cut apart each page to form piles of sentence strips by color. This would produce instant paragraphs. Remember I mentioned that it was an early September day? What I failed to notice on that particular day was the shift in wind direction. With eight sets of windows open wide on a very warm sunny afternoon, the wind began to blow straight into my classroom with instant gusts. Every strip of paper—an average of thirty to forty per student—gracefully floated to the opposite wall and out the open door of our classroom. We couldn't get the windows down fast enough. The damage was already done. Children passing in the corridors were stopping to gather the slips that had blown into the hall. That early in the school year, I wasn't familiar enough with the handwriting of each student to separate the hundreds of sentence strips. We looked like a picture right out of the auto assembly line. I manned the beginning and end of the line. One by one the children examined the strips, collecting the familiar ones. The strips that reached the end of the line unclaimed were resubmitted at the beginning and passed through the line again. Two good things happened that blustery day. The whole class learned a lot about everyone else's research, which gave them new ideas for their own. And I learned a valuable lesson about weather and innovative classroom techniques. We still use this method of paragraphing on windy days, but never with the windows open.

Paragraphing can be accomplished in a variety of ways. Some students might prefer rewriting the sentences into new paragraphs, foregoing the gluing and risk of wind damage. Regardless of the method used to put the paragraph together, many students return to the resources to look up additional information to help them make better sense of their paragraphs. The students are very creative, when it comes to devising ways of putting their paragraphs together.

Rethinking the Possibilities

Throughout each part of the research process, the most important event is acquiring new knowledge. The knowledge of the process—"how" to gather and manipulate the information—is of great value, but the most important factor in student research is the knowledge attained about the subject being studied. We never want to allow the process and mechanics of student research to occupy our time to the point where we lose sight of our real purpose. Students are reading, gathering, sorting, and arranging information in order to increase their knowledge in one area, so that it may be generalized into other areas and enrich their lives.

CHAPTER 7
Students as Writers

When they are completely satisfied with the paragraphs they have created, the student researchers enter a whole new phase of the research process. This new phase is the writing process. The students are now ready to look at the collected research information in terms of the final product.

The Writing Process

The writing process utilized with theme study is based on the research done by Graves and Calkins. Their books on writing were an inspiration and guided my thoughts about the writing process. The steps of the writing process are not strictly linear. Students move back and forth composing, revising, and editing, until they are satisfied with their end results. Regardless of what the final product consists of or what shape it takes, it will always contain an element of writing that will necessitate the writing process. Writing in the content area, as opposed to creative writing, requires the use of new types of sentences with different structures, vocabulary, and formats.

Rough Draft

In the area of content writing, the paragraphs in their glued, written, or "whatever" form, make up the rough draft. The rough draft is only the beginning of the final form. It is the place where the students can begin to look at their research results as a collective piece of knowledge. The rough draft can be as unpolished as the name implies, but to the young researcher it symbolizes an enormous accomplishment. The rough draft is a plateau where the students can rest and reflect. They put aside the research role and pick up the qualities of an author.

The rough draft can take so many different forms depending on the configuration of the final product. For instance, if the final product is a mobile with many pieces, then the rough draft would probably look like a miniature model of the final mobile.

Revision

Revision is the crucial part of the writing process. It is the part of the process that creates a better piece of writing. Without revision, the information would lack reflective insight. It is important for us to realize the important role revision plays in the quality of the children's work.

Revision means literally "seeing again." In order to help children, teachers have to be able to understand what students see in their writing and how they arrive at that place. Revision involves a writer looking at his or her written work as a reader (Smith, 1982). This gives the writing a new perspective. The student author is now looking at the total impact of the information collected piece by piece.

Revision is a personal matter. Personal interaction takes place between the rough draft and revision. As the students read what they have written, new ideas build on previous ones and revision takes place. The first draft is only the beginning of something brand new. In essence, the reason for revision is to discover new ideas, view a concept from a new perspective, rethink the possibilities, and change the writing to communicate new ideas and meaning.

Theme study involves writing in the content area, which is the most difficult kind of writing for children to revise. Content area information has not been experienced or created from a child's imagination. Therefore, higher-level thinking skills come into play when students revise their theme study rough drafts. They begin by rereading each sentence, and recalling the pieces of information gathered on their topic. Short connecting sentences might be necessary to relate pieces of information to each other. The students may see the need to obtain additional information to construct more precise meaning in the paragraphs. As they are revising the information, they may even see the need to cut away some collected pieces of knowledge that do not support the same main idea as the other sentences in the paragraph.

A characteristic of all children and their writing is their pride in what they initially write. Most children look at their first draft as their last draft. The ownership and pride of accomplishment gets in the way of any thoughts about revision. Teacher input is essential in the revision process. The amount of input seems to be the key to success. In order to achieve the right amount of input without damaging the student's confidence and feeling of ownership, a teacher must be extremely sensitive to the writer's needs. There are several ways to fulfill the students' needs without stifling their creativity.

Modeling, individual conferencing, and mini-lessons are a few strategies that are successful with students. Modeling and individual conferencing have been a vital part of the entire theme study, and the revision phase is no exception. Mini-lessons are utilized in those teachable moments that call for a little teacher input and are the result of a teacher's observation. After viewing several rough drafts and seeing the same need emerging, the facilitator would realize a strategy lesson was in order.

In the theme study on endangered animals, one student made each of the topic sentences for her paragraphs sound exactly alike. She wrote:

In this paragraph, I will tell you what the African elephant looks like.

In this paragraph, I will tell you what the African elephant eats.

In this paragraph, I will tell you where the African elephant lives.

This was not an isolated case in the classroom. There were several students struggling to write topic sentences for their paragraphs, and as a result they were turning out similar structurally redundant sentences.

Realizing which students were experiencing difficulty, I called them together as a small group and presented a mini-lesson on how to write topic sentences that would give unity to their paragraphs in an interesting way. As a group, we worked on each other's paragraphs by sharing ideas. This kind of interaction and support strengthens the bond between the students and lessens the feelings of inadequacy that the students might be experiencing.

The mini-lesson would be presented as needed, not planned in advance for a certain day. It could be given only to those who needed the strategy or modeled for the whole class. Mini-lessons should be concise, brief, and to the point. Facilitators should give a strategy, not direct the content of the students' paragraphs.

Many facets come into play during the revision process. Ownership plays a vital role in the students' motivation to keep improving their rough draft. Individual conferences are the key to communication and collaboration. Most children do not know how to revise a rough draft. Without having the contents of their paragraphs turned into a teacher-oriented product, students need to know the strategies that will help them revise a rough draft in their own words.

The realization that revising did not come as naturally to children as it does to most adults came as something of a surprise to me. For years, I had no idea how important it was to present strategies that would encourage students to revise their writing. After many individual student conferences, mini-lessons, and modeling sessions, I realized the fundamentally important role that revision serves in the theme study.

Editing

After the rough drafts of paragraphs have been revised and the student authors are pleased with the results, it is time to turn their attention to the mechanics and grammar. On the first day of school, the students in my classroom create a writing folder to accommodate all of their writing needs for the year. The writing folder contains many checklists and a page of proofreading symbols. As the students edit their writing, they all use the same common symbols to indicate problem areas.

- ⊋ Indent or new paragraph
- ᵥ∧ Insert or add something
- ℓ Omit or take out something
- ≡ Capitalize
- ⌐ Make a lowercase letter
- ◯ Misspelled word

Editing checklists help guide the students to look at many different aspects of their writing that might not automatically be seen as needing change. Editing checklists can be written to accommodate the needs of your classroom. Checklists can start out with basic skills and grow to meet the needs of the classroom with more advanced skills in grammar and mechanics. Adapting the checklists to the needs of the students throughout the school year serves as a good reminder of the progress they are making in their writing.

Self-Editing

The strategy of self-editing is an important technique for the students to learn to execute automatically. It is important for the students to learn how to edit their own writing to the best of their ability before they ask another person to edit it for them. This is part of the responsibility they assume for their own learning. They can use an editing checklist, which alerts them to needed corrections. Children, like adults, do not easily catch their own editing mistakes. It usually takes someone less familiar with the piece of writing to edit it well.

Peer Editing

Peer editing is a valuable exchange between two students. The peer editor becomes a reader and a word detective. As they read through the rough drafts of their friends' research reports, peer editors receive some additional writing benefits.

- They feel a sense of responsibility and purpose.

• They learn from reading the information gathered by another researcher.
• They see themselves as an important part of the classroom community.
• What they learn to look for in the writing of others will become apparent in their own writing.

When the peer editors have completed the job, their initials are written under the student author's name. This adds an element of accountability to the process of peer editing.

Writer/Teacher Conference

After the author and the peer editor have edited the writing, it is time for another one-on-one student/teacher conference. If the author and peer editor use different colored pencils to edit the piece of writing, then the teacher can distinguish the self-editing from the peer editing when reviewing the writing and assess both of the students' skills at the same time. For me, this is a time for teaching the mechanics and grammar of writing to each student in my class. The teacher gets a rare look into exactly what written language skills are present and lacking simultaneously. This is a perfect teachable moment that is custom-fitted to meet the exact needs of each student.

The conference can be conducted in any manner that is comfortable for the student and the teacher. I try to make editing conferences as private and isolated from the rest of the class as possible. When the students and I are having one-on-one conferences, I want the children to be aware of several things:
• They have my undivided attention.
• Their writing is important.
• They need to recognize the strengths in their writing.
• They can learn from their mistakes or omissions.
• Their writing has a purpose.

Editing is the time in the writing process when children should be encouraged about the mechanics that are present and acquainted with the ones that are omitted. The conference should convey a positive attitude toward the children's work, and this in turn will encourage and empower the student to grow in the weak areas of mechanics and grammar.

If the editing step of the writing process is treated as a time to make good work better, not a time to point out writing errors, students will eagerly seek the advice of their peers and teacher. They will view editing as a way of strengthening and perfecting their final product.

Editing will become a means of creating a richer, more valuable piece of writing. Students will welcome the input that helps them create the best final product possible.

Final Draft

The only business that remains is creating the final form. The rough draft at this point is a combination of added information, inserted words or phrases, deleted information, and a mass of editing symbols. Now the students begin to rewrite it in whatever format necessary to produce the final product. They use dictionaries, thesauruses, English handbooks, and any other resources necessary to the create a final product that is ready for publication.

Since the final product can take on several forms, it is impossible to describe the final draft of the writing in a specific way. The final draft is a culmination of the complete writing process. It has been organized and reorganized, revised, self-edited, peer edited, and conference edited, and is now ready for its original purpose to be realized. It is ready to be shared with an audience.

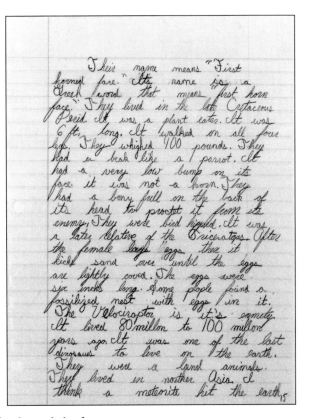

The Teacher as Facilitator

Where is the teacher while the research and writing process is taking place in the classroom? You as a teacher are everywhere! Every new part of the process is modeled by the teacher either through the actual participation or with an illustrated explanation on the chalkboard or overhead.

An illustrated explanation is a very effective tool. The maxim "one picture is worth a thousand words," is certainly true for children. During a brainstorming session or a discussion of any kind in the classroom, a sketch or drawing brings quick understanding in most situations. Children easily associate with illustrations. When we were discussing the final product for our endangered species theme, the students wanted to create a mobile, but they had great difficulty as a class trying to visualize the various sections and how it would eventually appear as a finished product. By illustrating it on the overhead, the class was able to create and revise the mobile image to make it appeal to the whole community of learners. This is what the final illustration looked like at the end of the session on page 70.

Endangered Species Mobile

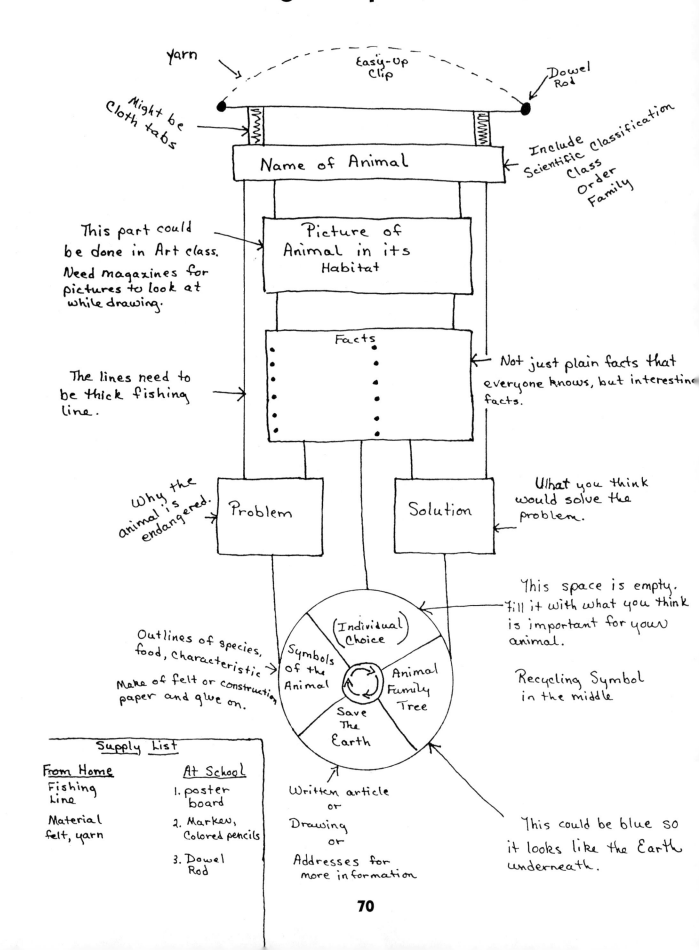

yarn

Easy-Up Clip

Dowel Rod

Might be Cloth tabs

Name of Animal

Include Scientific Classification
Class
Order
Family

This part could be done in Art class. Need magazines for pictures to look at while drawing.

Picture of Animal in its Habitat

Facts

The lines need to be thick fishing line.

Not just plain facts that everyone knows, but interesting facts.

Why the animal is endangered.

Problem

Solution

What you think would solve the problem.

This space is empty. Fill it with what you think is important for your animal.

Outlines of species, food, characteristic

Make of felt or construction paper and glue on.

(Individual) Choice

Symbols of the Animal

Animal Family Tree

Save The Earth

Recycling Symbol in the middle

Supply List

From Home	At School
Fishing Line	1. poster board
Material felt, yarn	2. Marker, Colored pencils
	3. Dowel Rod

Written article
or
Drawing
or
Addresses for more information

This could be blue so it looks like the Earth underneath.

70

Personal, one-on-one conferences are conducted whenever the need arises among the body of learners. The facilitator meets the individual needs of the researchers as they work their way through many different types of resources looking for the answers to their questions. As the researchers turn into writers, the teacher listens to the rough drafts and gives insight to new possibilities.

Our role as classroom facilitators is to ensure that all students are not impeded in their research by tasks or materials that are too difficult for them to understand on their own. We need to assist students in any area that they are unsure of in order to lessen the burdens that can plague the learning process. Tasks that might impede could be as simple as looking up a word in the dictionary or as complicated as using the *Readers' Guide* to locate a certain article in a periodical. Since the needs of the classroom are so diverse, we need to be able to change direction at a rapid pace in order to accommodate our whole community of learners.

On one occasion, while our class was deeply engrossed in researching a new theme, some visiting teachers entered the room to observe the children at work. As I was busily preparing the computer, searching for a specific article in a magazine, and pointing to several resources on my desk—in other words facilitating my classroom—one of the twenty-nine students became impatient waiting for a turn to speak to me. Usually the students reach out to the other students when they need help, but since there were other big people in the room, he approached one of the observers. To my surprise, I heard him politely ask, "Do you know how to use an encyclopedia?" The visiting teacher grinned and proceeded to be a facilitator.

As a facilitator, you must at all times endeavor to meet the individual needs of your students. It can be exhausting, but it is never bothersome or boring. To be needed is the reward of all teachers.

Community of Learners

The community of learners is really a combination of the children as researchers and writers, and the teacher as facilitator. Becoming a community of learners does not happen overnight. There is no way to put a time limit on it. It is created through mutual trust between teacher and students and among the students themselves. The students trust the teacher to give them the opportunity to have choices about their learning, and the teacher trusts the children to be responsible for those choices. The students trust each other to be kind, caring, and willing to share their knowledge and abilities. This creates an atmosphere where learning can take place.

There are other factors that contribute to creating a community of learners. Some of them are the same as the ones we looked at in the first chapter, when we focused on the differences between a theme unit and a theme study or cycle. Teachers have a different outlook on what they expect from the students in their classroom. Their goal is not simply to accomplish written mandated objectives but to become personally involved in each child's learning process. In almost all areas of the classroom life, there needs to be teacher-and-student collaboration. Theme study provides exactly what is needed to produce such collaboration. The children participate in planning and mapping out all the aspects of the theme study. Because they have so much input in the decisions involved in a theme study, they realize their responsibility to themselves, their peers, and to the teacher. The element of responsibility, not only to themselves but to their fellow class members, sparks the students into becoming a community of caring, sharing learners.

Rethinking the Possibilities

The whole concept of students as writers is more than just a process that creates competent authors. The confidence children gain while accomplishing the tasks of taking notes, creating sentences, arranging paragraphs, revising, editing, and completing a final draft is astonishing. The writing process provides an atmosphere in which pride and ownership can flourish with positive results. The process supplies the students with a means of communicating their thoughts and knowledge in a meaningful and purposeful manner. Communicating through the written word not only demonstrates their written language abilities, but it is tangible evidence of their accumulated and synthesized knowledge. To the students, it becomes a trophy of their learning experience.

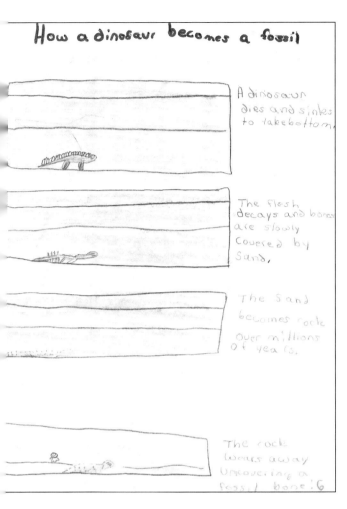

How a dinosaur becomes a fossil

A dinosaur dies and sinks to lakebottom.

The flesh decays and bones are slowly covered by sand,

The sand becomes rock over millions of years.

The rock wears away uncovering a fossil bone. 6

Samples of student work
at various stages in theme studies.

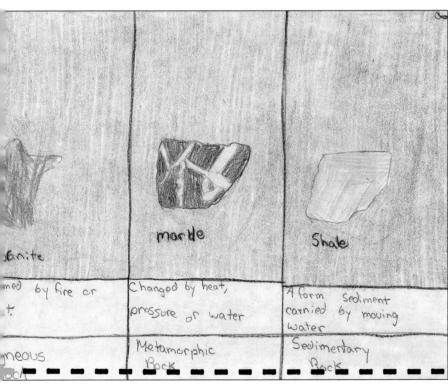

granite

marble

shale

...med by fire or ...t.

Changed by heat, pressure or water

A form sediment carried by moving water

Igneous Rock

Metamorphic Rock

Sedimentary Rock

CHAPTER 8
Students as Presenters

It is one thing to research and put together information in a written form or final product, but it is quite another to stand before a roomful of your peers and present what you have learned. Merely gathering the "head knowledge" of what is involved in speaking in front of an audience is no substitute for the real thing. Standing before an audience of your peers to expound on a subject that you have researched is mentally, socially, and physically demanding. This is especially true for children. Children have a lot to lose if what they do in front of their peers turns out to be less than what is expected.

• Mentally, the students must make preparations to present the knowledge obtained through their research in such a way that it can be understood by an audience of peers.

• Socially, they must present their material in a manner that is in accord with what the class as a whole considers acceptable conduct. Children notice small errors and bloopers immediately. Creating a community of tolerant listeners becomes an important part of classroom presentations. It is always prudent to remind the class that each of them will stand before the same audience. After a community is established among the learners, the social issue of oral presentations quickly disappears.

• Physically, the students, no matter how confident and prepared they might be, experience some anxiety about their upcoming presentation. This is a natural phenomenon for most adults, and it is certainly prevalent with children.

Preparing to Speak

There are many preparations to be made before the students present their findings to an audience. Their final product needs to be in its completed form. All of the research must be finalized in order for the researchers to study and understand their findings well enough to share them with an audience. At the completion of the final product, the student researcher needs to begin thinking about how best to present the final product.

The contents of the presentation are completely up to the presenter. There is no brainstorming session on what will constitute the presentation, but the students are encouraged to share ideas and draw from each other. This interchange with the future audience will help ease the burden of the social aspect when they are presenting. Every theme will be distinctly different as it is presented, because of the diverse subjects and final products, but even with all the differences that make up each theme study, there are some common characteristics that are found in most presentations.

Writing Speeches

Usually a speech is prepared to help guide the presenter through the presentation. Writing a speech that contains all the information that a student wants to share can be a considerable but rewarding undertaking. The students must condense all their research findings into a speech that conveys all the knowledge they want to share about the theme. They must decide for themselves how best to express the important information in a meaningful and comprehensible way. The length of the speech varies with the individual student.

Generating Checklists

Prior to presentation day, a whole-class lesson on delivering a speech is necessary. It is important to build confidence in the students by teaching or reviewing the characteristics that are present in a good speaker. At the end of the learning session, a checklist of things to remember can be brainstormed by the students. It might contain statements or questions that the students can ask themselves as they practice giving their speeches. A personal list of reminders reinforces the important qualities of a proficient speaker. Some of the questions might be:

1. Do I speak loudly enough for the whole audience to hear?
2. Do I speak clearly, so the audience can understand me?
3. Do I use some words too much, like: and, OK, so, etc.?
4. Do I look at the audience enough?
5. Do I look down at my notes too much?

This list of self-evaluating questions encourages the children to self-correct small public-speaking errors before they do it for real.

Rehearsing Speeches

The students might practice what they want to say with a friend to get some constructive criticism on what could be improved before the student presents to the whole group. Using their peers as sounding boards helps the students feel more relaxed about the impending presentation day. Many times the students ask to go to a lower-grade class to give their presentation before an audience that is less frightening than their peers. The students are also encouraged to practice at home with parents, guardians, or siblings. Another beneficial strategy is to say the speech in front of a mirror. With each rehearsal, the students gain confidence in themselves as speakers.

Composing Note Cards

After many rehearsals, the students become very familiar with the material covered in their speeches. But as with all memory work, there is always that one thought, idea, or fact that eludes the speaker. That is when a note card of reminders helps relieve the anxiety of forgetting a part and stalling the speech. Some students prepare index cards with reminders of important points that they want to make during their speeches, while others only jot down the points that were hard to remember during practice. The note card is a kind of security blanket for the novice speaker, and it enhances the speeches of the more experienced students by providing specific dates, crucial numbers, and other pertinent details that make the speech more interesting.

Coordinating Attire

Some of the students really get into the spirit of presenting, and they wear clothing that enhances their presentations. Over the years, the children have worn sailor hats when reporting on ships, and T-shirts with designs that depict some aspect of the theme. They have created costumes to wear over their street clothes, and worn jewelry or other coordinating articles. An antique aviator helmet was worn during a theme study on conflicts, but the best article of clothing, which served two purposes, was a sweatshirt worn by a girl named Becky, who was the daughter of a farmer. The theme study was animals. Because she lived on a farm and helped raise sheep, Becky quickly chose sheep as her expert topic. On the day of presentations, she wore a sweatshirt with a fluffy appliqué of a lamb on it. The front of the shirt had the head of the lamb with a bell around its neck; the back of the shirt was the back end of the lamb, complete with a dangling tail. Privately Becky and I cooked up a scheme that took the class by surprise. Becky waited to be the very last speaker. When she had finished her presentation, instead of thanking her audience for their attentiveness, she slowly turned her back to the audience (and the camera)and said, "The end!" The students loved it. The story was remembered and retold throughout the year. Theme study allows the community of learners to make memories among themselves, which creates a wonderful sense of camaraderie.

Creating an Audience Guide

A note-taking guide can be created ahead of time for use by the audience. A committee of students is responsible for creating the study sheet. It usually lists the names of the students and their areas of expertise. Ample space is left between each entry to allow for the notes to be taken as the students present their research information. This guide is not a necessity. Students can easily learn to take notes without a prepared sheet. The audience guide is a child-created organizational tool that was brought into being by a large class of thirty students. There were so many of them that they felt a need for a more organized method of compiling the information learned from their peers' presentations. Each class has created a slightly different type of guide, and the style may change from theme to theme. The student committee in charge of the guide interviews the rest of the class to get a consensus of what the body of learners as a whole feels is needed in the guide for that particular theme. The committee has responsibility for creating, typing, copying, and distributing the guide to their classmates before the presentation day.

SAMPLE AUDIENCE GUIDE

Ocean Notes

Movement: Waves
              Tides
              Currents

Description	Humpback Whale
Sailors	Sailfish
Maps	Flying Fish
Pollution	Sea Otter
Storms	Squid
Sunken Ships	Manatee
Hammerhead	Dolphin
Blue Whale	Bottle-nosed dolphin
Great White Shark	Angel Fish
Jellyfish	Moray Eel
Killer Whale	Starfish
Octopus	Whitetip Shark
Ray	Sea Horse

Preparing Visual Aids

Students often choose to use visual aids when they are presenting. Visual aids add strength to the presentation as well as support to the presenter, and come in all shapes and sizes. The students have made such items as charts, graphs, and diagrams, and they have also used borrowed articles.

During a presentation on the systems of the body, one presenter unrolled a large, very detailed chart of the lungs, which she used to explain the function of the bronchial tubes. As soon as she had completed her speech to the class, she called her mother, who promptly arrived to pick up the huge chart. As it happened, the night before her presentation she had visited her pediatrician for a routine check-up. While she was waiting in the examination room, she noticed a wonderful chart on the wall. She asked the pediatrician if she could borrow it for her speech, and he agreed on the condition that it be returned after the speech. The children were really impressed to have a real medical chart in our classroom.

Many other objects have been used as visual aids in my classroom, including live creatures. Most of the time models, pictures, or objects from home accompany the students when they share what they have learned from the theme study.

Setting

The setting is very important to the students. They want the environment to be appropriate and worthy of all the hard work they have done on their research projects. This becomes a whole-classroom community project. Committees are formed for various purposes, such as background scene, presenter table arrangement, prop design, and audio for the background sound. The students make decisions about every aspect and carry out their plans for creating what they feel is the proper setting for the theme. They utilize bulletin boards, classroom furniture, books, plants, and many other materials to design an original setting for the presentations.

Presenting to an Audience

On the day of presentations, a sense of nervous anticipation is felt throughout the room. It is much like the opening night of a play. The speeches have been prepared and practiced, the setting is complete, the audience has their guides and is ready to listen, and all that is left is to start the show. The students choose the order in which they present. They decide when the time is right for them, and they volunteer to be the next speaker.

Most times, I videotape the presentations. The camera is usually six to eight feet from the speaker, in the midst of the audience. A lapel microphone clipped to the speaker helps to create a better recording and it allows me to record as part of the audience, instead of being stuck in front of the other listeners, recording at close range. This creates a more comfortable, less intimidating environment for the children to share all they know with their peers.

On presentation day, I am not only part of the technical crew, but I am part of the audience as well. While taping the student presentations, I jot down any information that is factually questionable. The camera is placed on pause and time is taken after each speaker is finished to let the audience ask questions and digest the new information shared by the speaker. I ask questions along with the students. The student audience asks very good questions of the speakers. They are truly interested in learning about the subject of the theme. Any mistakes or misunderstandings about the material presented are cleared up before the next presenter begins. Most of the time the mistakes are minor, and they are usually the result of being nervous.

During one videotaping session, a girl named Lindsey reported that "The school protects your brain." The minute she was finished, her first words were, "I meant *skull* not *school*." Mistakes of this nature are quickly cleared up following the individual presentations.

When the audience is satisfied with their understanding of the material presented, the next student steps forward to present. Depending upon the size of the class and the regular activities of the day, taping oral presentations could take several days to complete. Realizing that the taping session might take several days allows the children to choose not only the order in which they speak, but also the day. This alleviates some unnecessary anxiety when children know ahead of time on which day they will be presenting. This important time of sharing should not be rushed. On the other hand it is not productive to have the students under stress for prolonged periods. The best way to judge the time limit of the taping session is to read the audience and act accordingly. You can easily tell when they are tired and need a break. Their fatigue will become visibly noticeable as their interest wanes.

At the end of each taping session, we have what we call "Mingle, Mingle" in our classroom. This is a specific time set aside to talk with each other and clear up any lingering misunderstandings or answer any other questions that may have arisen after the session was completed. The students go from one student to another talking about the theme and recording any additional information that they gather.

Following the Presentations

In the days after the presentation, many learning experiences take place. I always relate the final activities of the theme study to climbing a mountain. We reached the peak with exciting presentations, but we must come down the mountain before we have completed the journey. Closure is very important to any theme study. All the loose ends need to be neatly tied up to secure the learning experience. This is not to say that a particular theme will never be thought of again. Quite the contrary is true. You will find that no matter which themes your class studies, each theme is woven into the next. This is true because the children continually build new knowledge on the knowledge they acquired in a previous theme study.

The day after the taping is complete, the students participate in a class viewing of the video. As they watch the videotape of their theme presentation, they self-evaluate their performance. They regard the other students' performances as a kind of guide or indicator for the way they perceive their own effectiveness as speakers. It is difficult for children to watch themselves on television with all their friends without feeling some degree of embarrassment. With the completion of several tapings, they become better self-evaluators, which enables them to improve the next speaking endeavor. Throughout the class viewing, the community of learners offers positive remarks to their peers as a form of encouragement and support.

Learning from Peers

The benefits derived from a theme study can be of an individual nature that help a student to grow, or they may be in a form that is beneficial to the entire class as a collective group. Most of the time what is advantageous to one is advantageous to all. The strength of our community of learners depends on how well we learn from each other. Whenever children present orally in front of an audience of their peers, several benefits are derived from the experience.

First and foremost, it builds confidence. Giving a speech for an audience is a kind of interaction that builds up a willing child's confidence. A student's confidence determines the measure of success encountered in everyday living. If children have confidence that they can learn, then a great deal of learning can and will take place in their lives. The confidence that children possess needs to be guarded and nurtured to create the amount of self-esteem necessary for a successful and rewarding life in school. Self-esteem is sometimes created by the audience of peers without their knowledge. Authentic reactions to an oral presentation can boost the confidence of the presenter in a way that no teacher could ever accomplish through individual praise.

A few years ago, I came across one of those rare students who is extremely shy, and will exist in a classroom unnoticed by the community of learners unless the teacher makes a conscientious effort to keep him involved. Even with my help, this student was extremely withdrawn and preferred the life of an isolate in the classroom. He had virtually no confidence in his abilities and was reluctant to burden anyone with the task of helping him. Assessing his abilities was a difficult task because he provided so little information. He had been labeled lazy and non-caring in his previous years of school, and his mother agreed that the same was true of him at home. He was the epitome of a non-motivated person. I suspected that he might be a good reader, even though he never gave me cause to believe it from the small amount that he shared in the literature study group.

During our study of the human body systems, I remember the apprehension I felt as we prepared to present projects on the body organs. Each child had chosen an organ for the purpose of creating a project that would show the function it performed in the body. I was worried that he would not have the confidence in himself to present what he knew in front of all his classmates. I watched him day after day reading nonfiction books, encyclopedias, and magazines, but I observed very little writing. When I would ask how his project was coming along, he would respond politely with, "Very well." He was in charge of the ear. We had ordered old models of the body parts to examine and use as displays in the classroom. He took the old broken plaster of Paris ear model to his desk, studied it, and drew pictures from the encyclopedia every day.

Finally presentation day arrived, and he brought in a contraption made of old dried pieces of a two-by-four, a paper plate, a pencil, an round oatmeal box, a rubber band, and a Styrofoam cup.

Right away the children's attention was drawn to his table. They gathered around him to examine his project until the bell rang to begin the day.

As speaker after speaker presented their projects, I was sure he would choose to be last. As time passed another frightening thought occured to me. He was not only going to be last, but he was going to refuse to speak altogether. This was another one of those events that

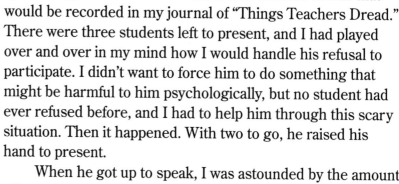

would be recorded in my journal of "Things Teachers Dread." There were three students left to present, and I had played over and over in my mind how I would handle his refusal to participate. I didn't want to force him to do something that might be harmful to him psychologically, but no student had ever refused before, and I had to help him through this scary situation. Then it happened. With two to go, he raised his hand to present.

When he got up to speak, I was astounded by the amount of knowledge he revealed through his speech. The contraption was a homemade ear that demonstrated how the vibration of sound traveled through the ear. As I paused the camera at the end of his presentation, I invited the students to gather round him for a repeat performance of his demonstration. The class was in awe of his accomplishment.

After that day, his confidence level was elevated enough to let him become a real part of our learning community. Theme study is a natural, authentic confidence builder because it allows the students to really get to know each other, not only on a social level, but also on an academic level. The students become colleagues with a like purpose: to *learn*.

Internalizing Information

Not only is their confidence boosted by presenting, but the students begin to internalize the information which enhances their lives and gives them the ability to remember what they learned. They begin to understand that learning isn't something you do to pass a test or fill in an answer on a piece of paper. It is a process that will continue to grow for a lifetime. By reiterating aloud what they have already recorded by written words and illustrations, they begin to make lasting impressions on themselves as well as their peers. As they share their own words with others, they begin to anchor the new knowledge in their minds.

Encouraging Cooperation

Today, in the business world, the key to a company's success comes from the exchange of ideas between workers and the management of the company. All ideas are considered valuable, and teams are formed to solve problems. The same premise applies in today's classroom. In order to prepare themselves to become valuable contributors to society, our students need to be able to work together and learn from each other. Forming committees to work on presentation projects such as producing the audience guide and creating a room setting generates opportunities for the learners to work cooperatively and collaboratively for a purpose.

Exchanging Ideas

In our study of endangered animals, the students decided that they wanted to share their information with the other children in our school. In order to accomplish their goal, they formulated a plan to establish listening centers all over the building. The activity included dividing into groups, drawing murals, writing scripts, recording the scripts on individual cassettes, and setting up listening stations in the halls. The sequence of the activity was clearly defined by the students in a whole-class brainstorming session. The problem that remained was how to form the groups. Thinking that they should group together by similarities, the students turned their attention to how their expert topics were alike. Some surprising similarities came to light as the children used their notes as tools for comparisons.

The following list is an actual list recorded from the session.

1. Types of animals (reptiles, mammals, insects, birds, amphibians, fish)
2. Architects or users (Do they build, or use what is available?)
3. Predators or prey
4. Land, water, or air animal
5. Warm-blooded or cold-blooded
6. Animals that help people or animals that harm people
7. Habitats

Looking at the list, the students narrowed down the possibilities by considering the number of listening stations they wanted to create. They wanted several stations, located in strategic positions for the greatest use by the student body. Because of their desire for the final product to have a number of stations, they began to eliminate the comparisons on the list that would allow only a couple of listening stations to be created.

The last choice on the list, Habitats, was chosen because of its diversity. From the variety of endangered animals that were chosen among the students, seven talking habitat stations were developed by the various groups. During the creation of the talking habitat stations, the students had to do some extensive research for the specific purpose of discovering more about the habitat in which their animal lived. They also had to be able to share their information and ideas about the landscape and its inhabitants with the other members of the group. Cooperative learning takes place when a group begins to make connections and synthesize the information into a finished product.

There are many ways to encourage the exchange of ideas among the students. During the initial brainstorming session, the class as a whole can decide on some specific activities that they want to use as the culminating activity of a theme study. These activities may involve the class as a whole or smaller cooperative groups. Depending on the project or activity, the number of students involved with each group will vary. There are many strategies for organizing group projects. Finding comparisons or contrasts among the expert topics, as with the endangered animals theme study, is a good place to begin. This is another instance when you as a facilitator only help the students as they search for connections and come up with categories that best serve their purposes.

Being Serious Presenters

The benefits derived from student presentations are innumerable. Presentations provide a mode of learning that has no equivalent. Authentic activities deliver the kind of experience that is necessary for real learning to take place. With real experiences, the students become serious about their learning, and they assume responsibility for it. The following humorous incident helped me realize how important the presentation part of theme study was to the students.

After a meaningful theme study on oceans, the class was preparing for presentation day. The whole class was ready to present what they had discovered about oceans in front of their peers and the camera. Since the students had investigated shells and the creatures that inhabited them during their study, they wanted to decorate the presentation table with a large shell arrangement. They placed the speaker's table in front of the fish aquarium with a huge ocean mural on the wall behind it. Ferns were moved from other parts of the room and placed in front of the speaker's table to represent seaweed. A cassette tape with the songs of the humpback whale was ready to play as an introduction to create the proper mood. The aquarium light was turned on and the classroom lights had been extinguished to produce just the right atmosphere for videotaping. The interior decorating committee that planned this creation had done an excellent job. The setting in which the students would give their well-prepared, well-practiced speeches was completed.

I began the videotaping the presentation by zooming in on the aquarium while the songs of the whales provided the background music. Because this was an atmosphere created by the children, they were as quiet as professionals on a movie set. The first student to speak, was a small, shy girl named Lora. She walked to the speaker's table and in a very studious manner began to share the knowledge she had learned during her research. Unknown to her, the cat from across the street had bounded onto our window sill. Because the students were so determined to keep their video free of any interruptions, they sat noiselessly watching the cat's every move. Being behind the camera, I didn't notice the cat until it leaped onto the bookshelf and began to walk at a leisurely pace toward the speaker's table.

My first hope was that Lora would be finished before the cat could disrupt the audience's or her frame of mind. That hope was quickly dashed as the cat jumped over the park bench and landed right in the center of the speaker's table. The day before we had reviewed the importance of good speaking skills, posture, hand gestures, and the seriousness of the oral presentations. The students knew that they were responsible for sharing as much information as possible with their peers, in order to make the theme study a success. In the light of what we had discussed, Lora had only one objective: cat or no cat she was going to share all the information she had gathered with her fellow learners. Lora went right on with her speech as the cat proceeded to look for a cozy spot to curl up in for a nap. In the process of walking around the table in search for that "purrfect" spot, the cat managed to knock from the table two huge scallop shells and a piece of coral.

After making an amazing amount of noise, the cat settled down near a big conch shell and playfully pawed the inside spiral. Despite the grand interruption, Lora never stopped presenting the material that she was determined to deliver. Finally she closed by thanking her audience for their attention. When I gave her the "off the air" sign, her hands immediately flew up to her face, and she said, "I didn't know what to do!" We all had a good laugh, and the cat was promptly escorted to the window. The windows were securely closed, and the recording session continued as planned.

That was the day that I realized how serious presenting was, not only to the speaker, but to the listening audience of peers. Oral presentation is a very important part of theme study. It is the students' Olympic event, the one they have been diligently preparing for since the day they began to browse in the resources.

Rethinking the Possibilities

The underlying current throughout the development of theme studies is purpose. Purpose drives the theme. All motivation comes from the purpose for which we begin, endeavor to accomplish, and complete a task. When the purpose has been defined, the students realize from the beginning that all of their hard work will not be in vain. It will not be collected and stacked on a shelf, but it will be recorded and displayed for all to see.

Because a theme study is driven by a real purpose, the final product and the new knowledge acquired through the study are the students' rewards. No bribes or external rewards are necessary to prod the students along through the process. The excitement felt about learning is the only prod they need to achieve their goals. The videotapes of the students' presentations are available to be checked out and taken home for an evening. In this way the purpose of the theme is shared at school and at home.

CHAPTER 9
Assessment and Evaluation

As a classroom teacher in a public school, I view the terms *assessment* and *evaluation* as different yet dependent upon each other in a continuous cycle. In the thinking process, we are constantly assessing information that we receive through our senses. We decide if the information is of importance or if it should be ignored. If the information is considered important, it is evaluated or judged as to its worth, quality, or significance. Then it is placed into a schema, a mental arrangement of ideas, as knowledge to be recalled or built upon.

In all respects, this is the way assessment and evaluation work, hand in hand. One is nothing without the other. Just as our senses determine the importance of the stimuli constantly bombarding our lives, teachers ascertain what information is significant and should be collected for each student. This decision will be different for every student in the class. The type of information gathered for each student will vary according to the individual needs and abilities of that child. After the information is collected, the data begins to grow, and a clearer picture of each student begins to emerge.

Assessing the information as a whole can give the insight needed to provide students, on an individual basis, with specific strategies to help them advance their abilities. Assessment views the importance of the information in a positive way. Abilities that a child exhibits are recorded and assessed for the amount of growth or progress implied.

The evaluation process involves examining and judging the worth, value, and quality of the collected information. To evaluate material that has been gathered, the teacher determines the degree to which the students accomplished their goals and the quality of their work. In my most idealistic dreams, I often imagine a day when we, in the public school sector, will be encouraged to provide evaluative narratives instead of calculated scores to reflect the abilities of the students. But for now, since we are still accountable for an accumulation of percentages for letter grades, a part of evaluation must include placing a numeric value on the students' work.

This does not mean that we should neglect to value the students' work in more productive ways; ways that can increase the abilities of the children. Evaluation should be viewed as a tool for empowering students to improve their abilities, not as a negative method of pointing out only the weaknesses displayed in their work. When evaluation is used to look for growth and progress, the whole concept of setting goals for the purpose of strengthening weaknesses can be utilized in the classroom.

The evaluator should take into consideration the students':

- individual strengths and weaknesses;
- progress shown from assessment;
- strategies already in place;
- attitude about learning; and
- previously accomplished goals.

The teacher can interpret the collected information, help the student set new goals, and decide what new strategies would be beneficial to the student. With all of these considerations in mind, grades or scores can be established for each student.

As teachers, we must never lose sight of the real reason for assessing and evaluating the students' abilities. The purpose is to become closely acquainted with the specific, individual needs of every student, so that learning can take place in an immediate, positive, and motivating manner. The cycle in which we collect data (assess), and make judgments (evaluate) is necessary to inform the teaching. Teachers benefit, because their instruction becomes very efficient. They know immediately, by evaluating the collected data, what the individual child needs as a strategy to strengthen a weak area.

Assessment and Evaluation Techniques

Anecdotal Records

Anecdotal record keeping is a very informative method of gathering student information. It is a simple procedure in which the teacher makes an observation about a student and records it for later use. The observation may relate to a student's learning process or social development, or it could be any piece of pertinent information considered important to the student's well-being. The most important aspect of anecdotal notes is that each piece of the information should be positive. When the positive side of anything is known, the weaknesses are revealed without being stated. In this way, you have a record of abilities and can fill in the deficits, rather that seeing all the weaknesses and having no idea what the child is capable of doing.

Anecdotal notes have another valuable purpose. They help create personalized parent conferences and staffing sessions. The enhancement that anecdotal notes provide to the parent/teacher conference contributes in a major way to the success of the conference. By sharing a child's own words, actions, or accomplishments, the parents are assured that their child is not just a number in a grade book but a vital part of the classroom community. The shared information expresses to parents the sincere interest that the teacher has for the students and their learning process.

These jotted-down, often unrelated pieces of information serve as markers or a base line for determining the progress of the students. The notes are very beneficial in providing needed information for

setting goals and encouraging each student's progress in all areas. Anecdotal notes are an excellent basis for ensuring correct information required when writing an academic referral, in such cases where a learning disability or physical disability is suspected. Since the notes are dated, a wealth of chronological information is available.

During a theme study, an extensive amount of information is constantly bombarding the teacher as she or he facilitates the learning process. Connections that are being made by the students become abundantly apparent. The way in which the students are gathering information and making new connections is invaluable to the teacher. By recording those connections as they occur, the teacher can set higher goals with the students as they progress through the study.

There are so many ways to record anecdotal records, and every teacher has a method that fits his or her needs. I carry a clipboard with all the information necessary to facilitate learning without having to return to my desk. The clipboard becomes my portable desk. At the beginning of each week, I put each child's name on the top of an individual adhesive mailing label. (There are many computer programs that enable you to print these labels easily.) I tuck the labels in the back of the clipboard for easy access. Because the clipboard is always with me, I can easily jot down notes without moving from the learning situation. By using adhesive labels, I can transfer them from the clipboard to their proper place in the child's file. Checking the labels at the end of the day puts into perspective which students I observed that day and which students need to be concentrated on the next day. This kind of daily observation and assessment helps the facilitator keep a constant record of all the students in the class.

Assigning Value

Assessment and evaluation take place in every area of theme study. It may be formal or informal. When by mandate it is necessary to give numerical values to the children's accomplishments, there are some crucial factors to remember.

- The scale should be simple.
- The reason for each value should be well defined.
- The students should know what each value means.
- The use of the scale should be consistent.

I use a very simple form for assigning numerical values to the students' work. The numbers and their values are understood by every student. The numbers 5, 4, 3, 2, and 1 represent the narrative equivalent of excellent (5), very good, or above average (4), good, or average (3), needs improvement, or below average (2), and failed to meet set standards (1). Those five numbers indicate the degree to which the students have accomplished their goals. Putting a numerical value on the children's work is successful if these things are true:

- The children are aware of the meaning that each number holds.
- The children know ahead of time what it takes to merit each of the different numbers.
- The children are aware of what is expected at each level of value.
- The children realize that the value they earn will be viewed either as a strength, or as a place to begin putting together strategies that will strengthen a weakness.
- The children view their mistakes as a learning experience from which they can gain knowledge.
- The teacher recognizes what is valuable, according to each student's individual needs.
- The teacher knows prior to evaluating what will constitute each numerical value and informs the students.
- The teacher realizes that the numerical value indicates only that an area is a strength or weakness and uses the information to implement individual strategies for improvement.
- The teacher is able to use the student's mistakes as a tool for learning and building new awareness in the student.

Theme Study Assessment and Evaluation

On my very first attempt at using theme study in the classroom, the topic the students picked was animals. From the first day, I was intrigued and engrossed with the process the students were using and the success they were experiencing. I became increasingly aware of how knowledgeable and motivated the students were becoming as the study progressed. I was caught up in the wonder of learning through themes to such a degree that assessment and evaluation never entered my mind. I had become so used to grading only the end product that my thoughts were completely focused on the process.

Then as the theme came to an end, I was faced with the shocking reality that the finished product needed to be evaluated for a grade. I had literally missed out on moments that would never come again. All the valuable information that could have been used to assess students' reading, writing, and research strategies was gone. I was left with a final product that was truly remarkable, but no record was available of their strengths and weaknesses exhibited along the way. There was no data to examine in order to provide strategies that would increase their knowledge and ability to do an even better job the next time.

Needless to say, the next theme was viewed from a completely different perspective. During the brainstorming session, due dates were posted on the students' calendars. Each time a due date arrived, I individually assessed and evaluated that part of the study. In this way, I had a record of valuable information that could be applied immediately to the individual child's learning process.

Theme study provides ample opportunities to assess and evaluate both formally and informally. The areas of student research, techniques for gathering information, the writing process, illustrations, the final product, oral presentation, self-evaluation, essay test, and portfolio decisions furnish the facilitator an abundance of information.

Student Research

In an informal assessment of observations, anecdotal notes can readily be recorded as the students are engaged in research. How a student organizes material and utilizes time can provide insight into which strategies are needed to help the student become a successful researcher.

Collecting Information

Whatever the technique used to collect information, the children should be aware of what is expected of them if a numerical value is to be assigned. In the case of notes taken on index cards, students should have information like this before they begin their note-taking:

- 5 - Key words and phrases only
- 4 - Key words and phrases containing small unnecessary words like: and, but, the, it, etc.
- 3 - Phrases containing unnecessary words that are repeated throughout the notes—if, for example, the subject were dolphins, and each note contained the word *dolphin*.
- 2 - Long phrases straight from the source and not in the child's words
- 1 - Complete sentences, straight from the source of information

The same type of evaluation would apply to other parts of the research. With each part, a different set of expectations would be necessary.

Writing Original Sentences from Notes
- 5 - Ideas stated in the student's own words and complete sentences
- 4 - A mixture of original sentences and phrases
- 3 - Some original sentences and phrases mixed with copied sentences from the source
- 2 - Mostly copied sentences, with a few original sentences
- 1 - No original sentences, only sentences copied straight from the source of information

Color Coding
- 5 - All sentences have been correctly categorized
- 4 - Most of the sentences are categorized, with a few exceptions
- 3 - Several sentences in some categories are misplaced in unrelated categories
- 2 - Every category contains many misplaced sentences
- 1- Sentences have been placed at random without any thought to categories

These are just some examples of evaluation expectations. You can build these only by knowing the abilities of your own students.

Illustrated Materials

Not all assessment and evaluation involves written material. Illustrations, diagrams, tables, or graphs may also be part of the final product. Expectations for illustrations should also be shared with students. It is easy for the teacher to discuss with the class those elements

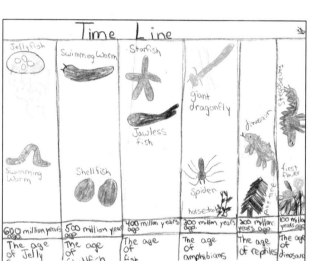

that help create an informative graph. To receive a 5 a graph might require the following ingredients: a graph title; a clear picture of what a graph represents; what data is being examined; how the data is being compared; easy understanding at a glance. When diagrams are being evaluated, the expectations might include proper labeling, a clear representation of the image being shown, an easily interpreted picture of a function, etc.

The illustrated material is treated like any other part of the final product in that expectations for evaluation should be established ahead of time to ensure that the learner is aware of the expectations.

Writing Process

Chapter 7 discussed students as writers. Each part of the writing process can be assessed for valuable information. The information can be viewed for the purpose of developing strategies that will improve the students' abilities to express their knowledge through their writing. From the rough draft to the final draft, assessing the students' abilities allows the teacher to encourage growth and provides the students with an environment in which they experience success.

The editing conference between the student and the teacher is a crucial place for assessment. This is the place where the teacher gets a clear and complete picture of the student's writing abilities after revision and self-editing have taken place. The teacher can assess the writer as a researcher, revisor, and editor. This is the place where writing assessment is utilized to praise the strengths and attend to the weaknesses of the individual student.

Individual expectations are easily outlined at the student/teacher editing conference. This is where the expectations for the evaluation of the final drafts are laid out. When the students leave the editing conference, they should have a clear picture of what they should accomplish in their final draft. These expectations will vary from student to student. The assessment data from checklists and anecdotal records will provide an accurate picture of each student's abilities. It is imperative to create a writing evaluation that can be adapted to all the students' needs without penalizing any one of them for abilities not yet acquired.

The following is one section of a writing evaluation form. This section deals with the mechanics of the writing.

- Capitalization— The student received a 4 in this area because all three of the capitalization skills were considered known abilities for that student. Failing to capitalize the title properly was more than likely carelessness on the part of the writer.
- End Punctuation—Since no other form of end punctuation was appropriate, the student put periods at the end of all of the sentences and received a 5 in that area.
- Commas— When this evaluation was conducted, the student was not aware of the need to use comma between the clauses of compound sentences. Perhaps this was pointed out for the first time in the editing conference, but the student had not utilized this new skill long enough to internalize it. The student was held accountable for commas in a series, after *yes* and *no*, and in dates, because she had prior knowledge of how they were used in writing. However, there was no need for the use of dates or the words yes or no in the final draft, so the abbreviation NA (not applicable) was placed in the assessment parentheses. As a result, the only use of commas that could be evaluated was commas in a series.

- Quotations—The same NA applies to a whole section that is not utilized in the student's writing. A numerical evaluation is omitted if the whole section is considered not applicable. In this way an evaluation can be done on each individual's abilities and only on what is contained in the final piece of writing.

WRITING EVALUATION

Name: _____

Date: _____

Kind of writing: _____

MECHANICS:			%	
Capitalization:	Beginning sentences (+)	4	90	B
	Titles (-)			
	Proper nouns (+)			
Punctuation:	End marks (+) ?() !()	5	100	A
Commas:	In a series (+)	4.5	95	A-
	Direct addresses (NA)			
	Yes and no (NA)			
	Dates (NA)			
	Between clauses of compound			
	sentences (-)			
Quotations:	Quotation marks ❏	NA	__	__
	Indent ❏			
	Commas ❏			
	End punctuation ❏			

Final Product

In order to assess the final product, the class decisions made during the initial brainstorming session will need to be reviewed. A simple checklist of brainstormed ideas gives a good representation of what components or pieces of the theme have been included in the final product. Each individual piece of the process has been assessed and evaluated as the theme progressed, and now it is time to look at the whole picture of the final product. Because of the many different kinds of final products, the final product will have to be assessed and evaluated on an individual theme basis. If the final product is a report, then an assessment and evaluation of its components—title page, table of contents, the paragraphs, and whatever else the students included during the brainstorming session—will need to be made.

RATING SCALE   Name: _____

	%	
5	100	Excellent
4.5	95	
4	90	Very good
3.5	85	
3	80	Average
2.5	75	
2	70	Below average
1.5	65	
1	60	Failed to meet standards

Date:_____

BODY SYSTEM EVALUATION   %
Notes (at least 60)   ___ ___ ___
Sentences (in own words)   ___ ___ ___
Color coding (categorizing)   ___ ___ ___

Diagrams (labeled)   ___ ___ ___

Title page   ___ ___ ___
Table of contents   ___ ___ ___
Project/experiment   ___ ___ ___
Speech (oral presentation)   ___ ___ ___
Essay test   ___ ___ ___

FINAL DRAFTS (content only)

System	(Description)	(Function)	(Disease)			
Circulatory	❑	❑	❑	___	___	___
Digestive	❑	❑	❑	___	___	___
Muscular	❑	❑	❑	___	___	___
Nervous	❑	❑	❑	___	___	___
Respiratory	❑	❑	❑	___	___	___
Skeletal	❑	❑	❑	___	___	___
" "	❑	❑	❑	___	___	___

COMMENTS:

If the final product is a mobile, those brainstormed components will be evident along with unique details and features that are the result of individual research. Once again, the expectations of the final product will need to be addressed, so that the students are aware of the expectations ahead of time.

 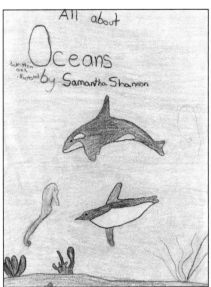

On a higher level of understanding, the final draft reveals how each child used the theme as a way of making new meaning by connecting new knowledge with prior knowledge. The final draft indicates the direction in which each child's interest was drawn by the amount of information found in any area of the theme. The final product reveals many different aspects about the individual child as well as the class as a whole. The teacher can easily see which concepts of the theme were understood and which ones left students teetering on the line between understanding and confusion. This assessment of the final product easily prompts meaningful discussions that will clear up many misunderstandings the children might have had at the close of the study. It can also lead the students into new areas and inspire new questions, which could ultimately launch a whole new theme study. In this way, the final product is not merely the end of the study, but the catalyst that stimulates the students to seek answers to new questions.

Self-Evaluation

Self-evaluation can be used at any time during the theme study. It can be used to assess what the children are thinking in terms of where they are in the research process, or as an evaluation of a completed task. After presenting orally to the class, my students take a few minutes to self-evaluate their performance. Children are usually very hard on themselves, because they do not know how to look at their strengths and weaknesses and achieve a balance between the two. They are automatically drawn to the weaknesses and feelings of inadequacy and failure. Making self-evaluation a regular part of the theme study helps children to acquire an understanding of the real value of examining their learning process. As they begin to see the value in self-evaluation, they will begin to use it in every area of their lives. As a tool, self-evaluation can turn failures into next-time successes. The children learn strategies for turning weaknesses into strengths.

Essay Tests

For me, one of the most exciting and rewarding evaluations of the theme study is the essay test. It opened my eyes as a professional educator as no other kind of evaluation ever did. Before my days of theme study, the only kind of tests I ever administered were fill -in-the-blank (with word lists usually included), multiple-choice, or true-and-false. A funny event in my life gave me the opportunity to view my testing practices and see just how educationally deficient they were.

When I was enrolled in a graduate program in pursuit of a master's degree, I was in testing situations on a regular basis. One night when I was agonizing over an upcoming exam, my husband asked about the nature of the exam. I told him that it would be a multiple-choice, using the traditional a, b, c, or d answers. The problem that plagued me was the way the choices were always written. One answer was always written so closely to the real answer that it easily tricked the test taker. I am the kind of person who can rationalize how almost any choice, with the right circumstances, could be the correct one. I am the type of test taker who reads too much into each question and suffers over the two best answers of each test question.

My husband quickly gave me a strategy to use. He said whenever that situation had arisen in his testing life, he used his watch as an answer indicator. He divided the face of his watch into four sections. Each quarter represented one of the letters of the multiple-choice test: a, b, c, or d. When faced with the dilemma of not knowing the answer, he would look at his watch to see which quarter the second hand was in. If the second hand was on the 5, the answer was clearly b. I was annoyed at his frivolous solution to my serious problem, but through his efforts to lift my spirits about the impending doom of my own test, he had unknowingly raised a question about multiple-choice tests and the students in my own class.

After much reflection, and observation of students' testing habits, I came to the conclusion that they did indeed use some ridiculous methods of choosing answers on multiple-choice tests. The fact of the matter was that the students who guessed, using whatever strategy they devised, could do as well as a student who had studied and was struggling to decide between the two best answers. On a true-and-false test, the chance of picking the correct answer was even better. They had a 50-50 chance of picking the right answer. Through all of this, I realized that I really didn't know what my students actually knew about any given subject. I couldn't be sure if the answer they had chosen was one of knowledge or just a "timely" guess.

When theme study became a part of my life as an educator, I realized that the tests that I had used for years were inappropriate for the type of information needed to evaluate a child's knowledge and abilities adequately. The essay test became the instrument used to peer into the minds of the children and see the connections that were being made.

Creating an Essay Test

This is not a tedious task. It is an exciting conclusion to an already successful study. Each theme study requires its own specific essay test that reflects the characteristics of that one study only. Even if the same theme is chosen again, a new essay test will be needed. This is true, because of the origin of the questions. Questions can be created by using several sources:

- Initial brainstorming ideas;
- Other avenues explored during the study;
- Information shared during oral student presentations;
- Concepts and conclusions revealed in the final product.

The test questions are created throughout the entire theme study. Because an essay test is customized to fit an individual theme studied by one class, it would not be applicable to another class even if the same broad theme were researched.

The way in which the test questions are asked is also a very important factor when creating an essay test. I usually refer to *Bloom's Taxonomy* to help me create a test that will extend children's thinking. The different levels of thinking require different elements of thought to take place in order to answer the questions.

Factual Knowledge

This requires the lowest level of thinking skills. This level simply asks the child to recall facts. This is the level of learning that is tested by fill-in-the-blanks, true-and-false, and, multiple-choice tests. These questions are included on the essay test, but they are by no means the only test questions.

- **1.** Name the 3 types of rocks.
- **2.** Identify the endangered animals in the picture.
- **3.** Tell 10 facts about the ocean.

Comprehension

At this level, the students are required to translate what they know into their own words and interpret their knowledge in terms of the connections they have made.

- **1.** Explain how each type of rock is formed.
- **2.** Summarize why the animals are endangered.
- **3.** Describe the ways in which the ocean moves.

Application

The level of application asks the students to show what they have learned through some method of demonstration.

- **1.** Illustrate how a volcano works.
- **2.** Construct the food chain of an endangered animal.
- **3.** Sketch the different kinds of water pollution.

Analysis

This level asks the students to take the knowledge they have and look at it from all different angles. They are asked to dissect what they know and put it into different forms.

- **1.** Compare and contrast two species of dinosaurs.
- **2.** Categorize the endangered animals by their habitats.
- **3.** Determine the factors involved in the creation of a hurricane.

Synthesis

The students are asked to do some creative thinking at this level. They must use all the knowledge they have gained in an innovative, creative way. These examples show how to give a student the opportunity to be creative with the theme study.

- **1.** Compose your own theory of why the dinosaurs became extinct.
- **2.** Pretend you are in charge of the world's environment. What changes would you make to save the endangered animals?
- **3.** Predict new ways the ocean could be used to help people in the future.

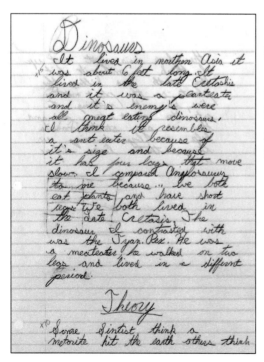

Evaluation

The last level of evaluation necessitates that the students put value on what they have learned by making judgments about it.

- **1.** Rank in order of most likely to least likely the scientific theories of how the dinosaurs died out and explain your reasons for the order.
- **2.** In your opinion, which is the worst violation made by people that endangers the ecosystem?
- **3.** Appraise how the ocean influences your daily life.

Another consideration when creating an essay test is the interaction of the community of learners. Since the theme study was a result of the efforts of all the students working together as a whole body of learners, it only seems appropriate to encourage that aspect as part of the essay test. Each theme lends itself to some activity that involves the students as members of teams working together toward one goal.

After completing the longest brainstorming session of the year, the students had accumulated a massive number of questions. The class decided that they needed to categorize their questions so they could make better sense of the information when it was gathered. The final result was four categories: Fossils, Rocks and Minerals, Earth Actions, Dinosaurs. Since the theme had so many different subjects to research, the children wanted to give the theme study a shorter name. Theme names were presented for consideration and voted upon. One little girl's entry was the acronym F.R.E.D. (fossils, rocks and minerals, earth actions, dinosaurs), which she pointed out was also the name of the father in the stone age family the Flintstones. The class was delighted!

The essay test I wrote at the end of the F.R.E.D. theme study is reproduced on page 104, but this was only half of the final evaluation. The students took this written test on one day, and were evaluated the following day on their skills as paleontologists.

A few weeks before the essay test, I prepared four Cornish hens for my family's dinner. After dinner, I stripped the excess meat off the bones of each hen, boiled the remaining meat off of the bones one hen at a time, and placed the hens in plastic bags filled with bleach and water to soak until the following evening. The next evening I removed the hen skeletons from the bleach solution and laid them out on paper towels to dry. By now, my daughter was thoroughly grossed out, my

F.R.E.D. ESSAY TEST

FOSSILS
1. Name 3 ways that fossils are made, and explain each of them.
2. Where are fossils found?
3. List at least 5 tools needed to hunt for fossils.
4. What do the fossils tell us?

ROCKS AND MINERALS
5. Name the 3 types of rocks and tell how they are formed.
6. Name 3 different tests used to identify rocks.
7. What are rocks used for in the world? Give 3 examples.

EARTH ACTIONS
8. How does a volcano work? Illustrate.
9. What good and bad things happen when a volcano erupts?
10. What is an earthquake?
11. How are earthquakes measured?
12. What is a fault?
13. Label the 3 layers of soil? Diagram.
14. Where does soil come from?
15. Name 3 colors that soil can be?
16. Contrast the particle size of sand and clay.
17. What is humus?
18. What kinds of things can damage soil? Name at least 3 things.

DINOSAURS
19. Describe your dinosaur by telling something about each of the following: When and where it lived; its size and habitat; what it ate; and who its enemies were.
20. What animal that is alive today resembles your dinosaur?
21. Compare your dinosaur to another.
22. Contrast your dinosaur with another.

THEORY
23. Name 3 common scientific explanations for the extinction of dinosaurs.
24. Now create a brand new theory of your own, using all the information you know from your study of F.R.E.D.
25. How do fossils help us today?

husband was annoyed about the inconvenience on the kitchen counter, and I had dried out hands and ruined fingernails. My son, however, was extraordinarily intrigued.

But it was all worth it. I counted out a sandwich bag for each child in my room, separated them into four piles, and marked each pile with one of the letters of F.R.E.D. Each of the four letters represented a team. One hen skeleton was distributed among the different bags for each team, so that each child would have several bones, but the team had one whole hen. Then I mixed up some plaster of Paris and dropped enough in each sandwich bag to cover the bones. I closed the tops and set the bags aside to harden.

The next day I met the children at the door of our room and let them pick a sandwich bag as they entered the room. They were well prepared for a day at a "dig site." They had each brought some kind of tool. There were hammers, screwdrivers, picks, pieces of cardboard to protect the tables, and brushes. I provided the skeleton books for bone comparisons. They matched the letters on the bags until each team was assembled. This was like taking a field trip within the classroom.

As the hammering began, I walked around the room to observe and listen to the interaction. The language the children were using was exhilarating. These weren't children playing a game or pretending to do something. They were serious students engaged in something they valued and found meaningful. The only clues I had given them were that it was an adult animal and each team had one whole animal of the same kind. The following are bits of conversation I recorded as the children worked.

"You know how smooth your bone is? This one is like that, too."

"I just think this is complicated, because one bone is next to another and then another. That's probably how it is when a real animal dies. Its bones just pile on top of each other."

"I think we need safety goggles!"

"Now I think this might be a leg bone. See the knobs?"

"I think mine might be a backbone, because it has that little edge on all the pieces."

"I've got two bones out, and they look alike. Same size, same shape, same knobs."

"What could it be?"

"Well, all we have are four bones so far. It could be almost anything."

"A mouse?"

"No, I don't think Mrs. Strube would handle a mouse. They're dirty you know. Besides this bone is too big for a mouse."

"But it could be a rat."

"No, I saw a skeleton in this book of a rat, and it didn't look like this at all."

"This bone looks like a whisker, but whiskers aren't bones."

"When I began to remove this bone, I thought it was going to be a little bone, but it turned out to be a big one."

"I found some little pieces of fur near the bone. I think it is a mammal."

"This bone measures about 3 inches. I think it is a rabbit."

"That rounded bone could be part of the rib cage, but the animal must be really small."

"These bones are alike, only yours is a tad longer than mine."

"We haven't found a skull yet."

"Wow! Look what I found. A hip bone or a shoulder blade.
This is going to be tough."

"This is like unraveling a mystery"

When all the bones had been found, the students began to move from group to group

observing what the other groups had turned up. As a result of the bleaching, some of the bones were more dissolved and detached than others. Only one group had a back completely intact. Each group began to pool their knowledge by sharing with each other.

We came together to compare our collective knowledge in order to identify the mystery animal. For this whole group brainstorming session, we divided the overhead transparency into three columns.

THE ANIMAL HAS:

In the first column, we listed what we knew about the mystery animal. In the second column we drew conclusions about the animal. What isn't it and why? In the last column, we wrote what it could be. The children decided that all of those choices were too big to be the correct animal.

The Animal Has	What it is Not and Why	Theory
a spinal cord		goose
	rabbit - neck is	
3-inch leg bones (2)	too long	duck
	frog - leg bones	chicken
small body and legs	are too big	
		turkey
no skull	mouse - back-bone is too wide	
no feet	rat - most bones too small	
long neck, many bones		

The most interesting conclusion came from a student who was connecting the knowledge from the study of dinosaurs with the facts of our unknown skeleton. The student concluded that the animal's structure resembled tyrannosaurus rex with its big back legs and all the other small bones.

The final column was used to synthesize all the gathered information and develop a theory about the skeletal remains. These were the three theories that the whole community of learners decided on together. Because of the two big leg bones, it probably walks on two legs. It resembles common poultry and water fowl. The skeleton probably belongs to a kind of adult chicken that doesn't get very big.

The final brainstorming session was very rewarding and successful. An enormous amount of higher level thinking took place on the day of our "dig." The children learned that every observation was valuable, no matter how insignificant it might seem at the time. While digging with his group, Irah heard a boy in another group ask, "I wonder why none of the teams has found a skull? We could really identify it if we had the skull."

Irah with a laugh in his voice said, "Maybe they were all chopped off!" Later, after the animal was identified, I reminded him of what he had said. Since I had indeed purchased the hens at the supermarket, that is exactly what had happened.

Even though our room resembled a giant chalkboard tray, the day was a tremendous success. There is no substitute for the opportunities that an essay test opens up to the teacher. When the two days of tests were finished, I had a complete and comprehensive record and an understanding of each child's knowledge, abilities, and amount of growth made during the theme study.

Rethinking the Possibilities

Theme study provides a multitude of assessment and evaluation opportunities for the classroom teacher. With every activity, the students provide an abundance of valuable information that reveals their strengths and abilities. From informal observation to a formal evaluation with an assigned value, the facilitator accumulates a large amount of pertinent information on each student. This valuable information provides the means by which the teacher can adjust or create meaningful strategies for building a curriculum that brings success to each child. The assessment and evaluation process tends to drive the curriculum of the classroom. Those concepts that are deemed important enough to evaluate are the same concepts that are included in the curriculum.

CHAPTER 10
Classroom Management

We see and hear the term *classroom management* in much of the educational environment. *Management* sounds like a buzz word right out of a corporate business meeting. Teachers, however, do not manage people and machines for the sole purpose of producing a product for profit. Teachers manage children and the environment in which they learn. The management of a classroom is not a job that can be taken lightly. It can be the key to success or the instrument of failure. Too much management in a classroom can become so overwhelming that it consumes the learning time. Too little management may destroy the learning environment to such an extent that all learning is halted. Learning is stifled by a chaotic environment as well as a rigid one. When your curriculum revolves around a theme being studied, classroom management and teaching blend together into one successful learning experience. When classroom management promotes responsibility, accountability, and a sense of community among eager learners, the right balance has been reached. Classroom management can be thought of in three broad categories: managing the environment, managing the curriculum, and managing record keeping.

Managing the Environment

In Chapter 4, we discussed the importance of creating with the students an interesting and accessible environment where students can conduct their research. It is just as important to maintain that learning environment on a daily basis.

Daily Responsibilities

In all aspects of life, some basic principles hold true. If you want someone to take care of some property, you put them in charge and empower them to be responsible. This principle applies to children as well. When you have a set of books, an aquarium, an expensive model, a computer, or any other kinds of classroom materials, it is impossible for the facilitator both to individualize and maintain a room full of equipment with any degree of quality. There is simply too much to take care of. The burden of responsibility must be spread out among all the learners in the classroom community.

Each child in my classroom is responsible and held accountable for one or two daily jobs that help maintain the classroom in good working order. The last fifteen minutes of the day are devoted to completing the designated jobs. In that time, the fish are fed, the computer is turned off and covered, the learning centers are straighted, volumes of the encyclopedia are collected and alphabetized, the paperback library is arranged by the class librarian, the overhead projector is unplugged and the cord wrapped neatly for night storage, plants are watered, the floor is swept, and notes or papers are distributed to take home.

During the day, other jobs are required to keep the classroom running smoothly. The attendance slip is clipped to the door, the door is closed when hall movement becomes disturbing, the door is answered and messages are delivered to me, the math papers are sorted by page number, and learning center sign-up slips are replaced.

The ownership the children feel for the classroom comes from the pride they receive from a job well done. Jobs are not assigned to the students. They go through the same process that an adult would follow when seeking employment. A list of room jobs is brainstormed by the class. Then the list is typed and posted for review. The children study the list and apply for the job they desire by submitting a résumé. A number, known only to me, is placed on each résumé instead of a name. An elected committee reviews the résumés and picks the applicant they feel is best for each job. For any jobs with two or more applicants, the children who were not "hired" go back to the job list and submit a new résumé to the committee. This process continues until all the students have one job. The remaining jobs are then open to all the students again through the same process.

> **Rt. 2 Box 223**   **SS# 488-96-8059**
> **Hannibal, MO 63401**
>
> I'm applying for the film center position. I'm a good worker and the center will be as clean as a mansion.
>
> **Education**   Attended The Little Red Caboose, Hannibal, MO Attended Oakwood School, Hannibal, MO
>
> **Experience**   WEe Care Daycare, Hannibal, MO Rita Smith, Supervisor
>
> **Skills**   Computer & Organization
>
> **References**   Marie Million, Quincy, IL Maria Mundle, Hannibal, MO Murl Smith, Hannibal, MO
>
> I hope you will hire me for the film center.

After the initial jobs are chosen at the beginning of the year, a job-training program goes into effect. For example, if a child wanted to be responsible for the computer but wasn't as qualified as another student, then the less qualified child could chose to be an apprentice to the qualified child and learn the techniques of computer care. Because of the training, the student apprentice would qualify for the computer job the next time. In this way, every job is an obtainable goal.

There is nothing new about jobs in a classroom. The difference lies in the attitude and method in which the jobs are attained. The choice behind the job selections fosters ownership, pride, and responsibility in the community of learners. The following anecdote illustrates how the children view their jobs.

Since the children change jobs about once every five weeks, they get to observe their predecessors on the job. From those observations, many of the students demonstrate more responsibility in the same job. This was the case with Erin. Her job was to answer the door when someone knocked. A few days after she started her new room job, a knock was heard across the room. She quietly slipped from her table and answered the door. At the door were two first-graders

who had come to read to our class. I was in a literature study group at the time, but I overheard Erin's whole conversation with the visiting children. She said, "May I help you?" They explained that they were there to share a book out loud with us. Her gracious response was, "I'm sorry. We have a literature group going now, but if you come back in thirty minutes, we should be finished." They agreed to return half an hour later.

Erin wasn't part of the literature study group that was in session, but she knew that the literature time was too important to interrupt. She made the judgment that the readers could easily return later. She always took the notes from the delivery child, brought them to me, waited for a written or verbal response, and returned to the door to deliver the reply. Normal interruptions from outside the classroom were almost eliminated. She set a new precedent for all the students that would follow her in that job.

The few minutes spent by each student each day not only keeps the room in good working order but promotes a sense of classroom pride. The students assume ownership of the environment, and all the small daily events that tend to interrupt learning in the classroom do not distract or break the concentration of the learners.

Managing the Curriculum

When the room environment is in place and the responsibilities have been delegated through classroom jobs, the teacher can focus more time on the curriculum. This allows more opportunities to individualize and facilitate the theme study.

Daily Schedules

Daily schedules help the curriculum become one continuous learning experience, while providing the students with their own personal agenda for the day. At the end of each day, I write a new schedule of the events that will take place the following day. When I begin to plan for the next day, my thoughts are not fragmented by page numbers in subjects like spelling, English, reading, etc. I see the new schedule as a continuation of the learning that took place that day.

The schedule serves as a daily reminder of the activities and due dates within the larger picture of the theme study. Before the school year begins, I create five schedules that reflect certain breaks at the specific times when the students are out of the regular classroom and involved in special activities, such as gym, music, art, and library. Since those special sessions do not occur at the same time every day, a schedule for each day of the week is needed. I make copies of the blank daily schedules and fill in the blank spaces with the events appropriate to each day.

The students pick up a new schedule each day as they enter the room. After they have socialized, sharpened pencils, and taken care of lunch decisions, they begin to individualize their schedule. They highlight the part of each section that applies to them. Many of the children place numbers by the unfinished activities to prioritize their day in

DATE:		STORY STATUS	
		Day #1	Rehearsal
LEADERS:		Day #2	Pre-writing
		Day #3	Rough Draft
FRIDAY		Day #4	Self-Revision
8:30-8:45	SSR	Day #5	Team Revision
8:45-9:00	CLASS MEETING	Day #6	Self-Edit
9:00-9:30	LANGUAGE ARTS	Day #7	Peer Edit
	1.	Day #8	Conference
	2.	Day #9	Corrections
	3.	Day #10	Final Draft
	4.		

```
9:30-10:30   ART
10:30-11:30  MATH:        PG __-__;       (EX __-__)      (WB__)

11:30-11:50  ORAL READING:    _____
12:25-12:30  LUNCH
12:25-12:30  REST ROOM

12:30-2:00   LANGUAGE ARTS      1.
                                2.
                                3.
                                4.
                                5.

2:00-2:20    RECESS
2:20-3:00    SCIENCE/SOCIAL STUDIES:   1.
                                       2.
                                       3.
                                       4.
                                       5.

3:00-3:10    JOURNAL
3:10-3:15    CLASSROOM JOBS

HOME ASSIGNMENTS:       1.
                        2.
                        3.
```

order to meet due dates. Since math is individualized, they each bring their schedule with them during their individual lesson and fill in the blanks with their new assignment. The students are also in charge of their home assignments. They evaluate their progress at the end of the day and decide what they need to work on at home. The schedule serves as a home reminder as well as a classroom reminder.

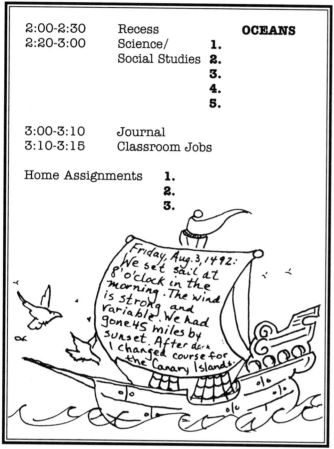

2:00-2:30	Recess		**OCEANS**
2:20-3:00	Science/	1.	
	Social Studies	2.	
		3.	
		4.	
		5.	
3:00-3:10	Journal		
3:10-3:15	Classroom Jobs		

Home Assignments 1.
    2.
    3.

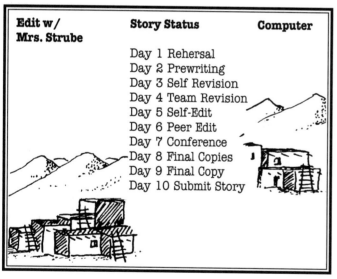

Edit w/ Mrs. Strube   **Story Status**   **Computer**

Day 1 Rehersal
Day 2 Prewriting
Day 3 Self Revision
Day 4 Team Revision
Day 5 Self-Edit
Day 6 Peer Edit
Day 7 Conference
Day 8 Final Copies
Day 9 Final Copy
Day 10 Submit Story

Daily schedules function as daily guides, as well as vehicles of learning. A vast variety of material can be shared at the bottom, top, and along the sides of the schedule. Art work heightens the enthusiasm of the learner. Some of my schedules have even become "collector's items!" I sometimes use schedule drawings to invite the children to investigate new realms of the theme study. Sketches can also be used to increase understanding.

During an inquiry time of a Native American theme study, I used the margins of the schedules to invite students to explore different aspects of the culture. Sometimes, I insert higher-level thinking puzzles or bits of information that will answer questions that we asked the previous day.

The schedule also provides a means for gathering information from the students. A survey or questionnaire might be necessary for record keeping purposes. Or the schedule could be a secret ballot of a classroom activity. It can be a tool to encourage the students to share information with each other, which fosters a more caring relationship among the community of learners. During the Endangered Animal theme study, one of the endangered animals appeared on the schedule each day. The children were to seek out the expert on that animal during the day and gather information for later use. The daily schedule also provides a means of communication between the teacher and the students on days when the teacher is away from the classroom.

The daily schedule has the capacity to inform, evoke enthusiasm, encourage cooperation among the learners, establish communication between teacher and student, and promote higher-level thinking. This type of scheduling serves a variety of purposes, all of which are essential to the learners.

Class Meetings

Conducting class meetings is a way of sharing knowledge and experiences among a group of peers. Some of our greatest creative ideas form during class meetings. The truly great ideas never come from just one child. They are always a combination of ideas that emerge within minutes after the initial suggestion that inspires them. The class meeting is conducted in a relaxed atmosphere that encourages everyone to share their thoughts. When I began conducting class meetings, I did it for the purpose of explaining or answering questions about the schedule for the day. That took only a couple of minutes. From that humble beginning, our class meeting rapidly grew into whole-group discussions about the weather that caused the snow, hungry people who need our help, the type of bird that was roosting on the corner of the school building, or whatever topic that was on the minds of the students. An incredible amount of incidental learning takes place when the students are interested and concerned about the world in which they live and are willing to share their knowledge and ideas with each other. The diverse backgrounds and environments of the students give new and different perspectives on the topics discussed at the class meeting. The meeting generally sets the tone for the day.

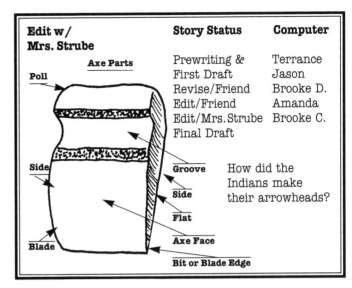

Edit w/ Mrs. Strube	Story Status	Computer
	Prewriting & First Draft	Terrance Jason
	Revise/Friend	Brooke D.
	Edit/Friend	Amanda
	Edit/Mrs. Strube	Brooke C.
	Final Draft	

How did the Indians make their arrowheads?

Axe Parts: Poll, Side, Blade, Groove, Side, Flat, Axe Face, Bit or Blade Edge

Personal Student Calendars

Each month, the students receive a personal calendar to record all the theme study due dates and other important information. The calendar entries may include contest mailing deadlines, days off from school, birthdays of famous people or relatives, local extracurricular events, classroom events, or any event that is important in the life of the student. The students refer to their calendars frequently, which helps them to be organized and able to meet their goals on time. Personalized calendars create a sense of responsibility within each student for the management of their own assignments.

BIRD LANGUAGE

Birds ues their voices more often than any animal except for human beings. Baby birds learn to sing by imitating adult birds, the same way humans learn to talk.

Becoming a Bird: Tip No. 1
• What color is it?
• What marks does it have and where are they—on the breast, wings, head, or tailfeathers.

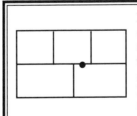

Begining at the dot, draw a continuous line that crosses every segment of line exactly once! Good Luck!!!

(Hint: There are 15 segments.) At 12:30, I will give you another hint.

Theme Study Binders

From the beginning of the theme study to the end and sometimes beyond, you will create and collect a large quantity of materials. Keeping all the different kinds of theme materials organized can take up some valuable time. A simple three-ring binder provides immediate organization and easy access to the theme materials. I create several sections in the binder by inserting pocket dividers, which allows me to organize the theme by including a section for planning, resources, theme study process, collected information, and test materials. At left are some suggestions for items you might include in each section.

Creating theme binders can serve two purposes. First, the theme binder provides organization for the present. The binder grows with the theme and is utilized to record what is developing as the theme progresses. It becomes a useful tool for maintaining long-range goals which you can refer to when making daily goals. It stores theme information in a central location so that you can quickly access it to help students with their research. Secondly, the theme binder can be a source of information for the future. It easily becomes a teacher resource for use in facilitating new themes along the same lines or reviving old ones to focus on different concepts and core competencies.

Managing Records

There are so many phases and activities involved in a theme study, it may seem that record keeping alone would be extremely time consuming. In fact with the use of checklists, anecdotal labels, analytic evaluation forms, and parent information forms, you can assess, evaluate, record, and report the child-centered information with ease.

Checklists

With a list of the students in your class and a basic all-purpose grid or chart, a personalized classroom checklist form can be created and used for various purposes throughout the entire year.

This kind of checklist can be used for everything from attendance to recording the progress of each child during the theme study process. The empty spaces provide enough room for a check, value, percentage, or grade. It allows you to evaluate an individual or the whole class at a glance.

Anecdotal Labels

The mailing labels give you a way of recording the students' spontaneous actions, thoughts, and ideas as they work through the research process. The labels are easily placed in the child's personal folder or section of a class assessment book at a later time.

Analytic Evaluation Forms

When examining the different parts of the theme study process, it is helpful to create an evaluation form that gives an overview for each individual student. This type of form gives a good picture of the student's strengths and weaknesses, which provides insight about strategies needed for specific parts of the process. It is also an excellent instrument for evaluating the students' research process, which can be shared with the parents. Parents easily see how well their child understood the process. How you create an analytic form will depend on what part of a child's learning you wish to analyze.

Parent Information Forms

Since the many different elements of theme study research take place mostly in the classroom, it is very important to keep parents involved and informed. About once every two weeks, I send home a parent information form with each student. It informs parents of the children's progress with grades and evaluation values on the front

Dear Parents,

I will be keeping much of your child's work at school in his/her personal portfolio. If at any time your child's grades fall below average, I will contact you immediately.

These grades reflect the progress of your child in recent days. Please look over the attached papers and ask your child about the assignments. The work that generated the grades written in the boxes is stapled to this sheet. Grades that appear in parentheses were generated by work that is either in a spiral notebook, or portfolio, or it has been made into a booklet. You are welcome to view these papers at any time. All of the saved work will be sent home at the end of the school year. If you have any questions concerning your child's work, use the back of the grade sheet for comments and give it to your child to return to me. I will respond to your questions as soon as possible.

Sincerely,
Mrs. Strube

PLEASE CUT ALONG DOTTED LINE AND RETURN

MATH _____ ❑ ❑ ❑ ❑ ❑ ❑ ❑ ❑ ❑

ENGLISH _____   SEE ATTACHED PAGE

SPELLING_____ ❑ ❑ ❑ ❑ ❑

CURSIVE_____ ❑ ❑ ❑ ❑ ❑

SOCIAL STUDIES: THEME (_____)

SCIENCE: THEME (_____)

READING _____ ❑ ❑ ❑ ❑ ❑ ❑

The / means your child failed to turn in the assignment.

of the form and a personal narrative derived from the anecdotal records on the back.

Another way of informing parents is by sending home a classroom newsletter. The students are great at describing the activities and studies going on in the classroom. There are many computer software programs for children that allow a class to create a newsletter, but a typed or handwritten student newsletter is appreciated by parents just as much.

Reflections on the Chapter

It is very difficult to balance the management of the environment, curriculum, and record keeping tasks in the classroom. If any one of the three aspects of management is neglected the consequences can be disastrous for both teacher and students. Encouraging the community of learners to become responsible for their classroom and the activities that take place within it is the key to balancing the different parts of classroom management. When the teacher and students share the burden of responsibility, the load is lighter for everyone.

The Discovery Log

September Issue   Rm... 108

Titanic

The Titanic was a very elegant ship that sunk because it hit an iceberg. It was 8 stories high. They built it to be unsinkable, but when it hit the iceberg it ripped a big hole. The water filled too many compartments, and it sank. Women and children were saved in the life boats. They said it was lost forever, but in July of 1986, Robert Ballard found the Titanic. It was the biggest ship made in the world.

By Stephanie Yohn

Shells

In room 108, we are studying shells. Shells are fun to look at and put into similar groups. There are many different kinds. In our collection, we have mollusks, a sea urchin test, a sand dollar, conch shells, snail shells, and scallops.

By Erin Aylor

Under the Sea

I wonder what the ocean holds,
Fish and shells, sunken ships of old,
Whales and sharks and jellyfish too,
I'd like to see them all, wouldn't you?

By Erin Otten

Fish Tank

There are many things in our room, and one of them is a fish tank. We have 14 fish in our tank. We have 3 Neon Tetras that glow in the dark, 4 Zebras (2 black and 2 yellow), 3 Fantailed Guppies with colorful tails, 1 pretty purple Beta, 2 unknown fish, and last but not least, our algae eater. It is black and gray and about 6 inches long. They are peaceful.

By Amber Park , Crystal Warren

Whales

There are all different kinds of whales. The largest whale is the Blue Whale. It grows up to be 102 feet long. They eat plankton and shrimp. Here is a chart of whales.

Name	Length
Blue Whale	102 feet
Fin Whale	82 feet
Bowhead	65 feet
Sei Whale	58 feet
Minke Whale	33 feet
Killer Whale	32 feet

By Chris Harlow
Bryan Hawkins

Rain Forest

Did you know that there are over 1,000 types of trees in the rain forest? There are many types of birds, for example parrots. There are all kinds of animals. Some people are burning down the rain forest. We think the President of the United States should do something about it. Many animals are becoming endangered.

By Irah Howe
Bobby Walden

Children Visit From the State School

On Friday, September 25, 1992 the children from the state school came to Oakwood School. Mrs. Strube's class and Mrs. Taylor's fifth grade did activities with them. We had a scavenger hunt in the front yard of the school. We had wheelchair races in the gym. At the end they furnished soda, chips, and dip. There were seven kids from the handicapped school. Rocky had a communication board that was really neat. We had a wonderful time with them.

BY Krissy Willett
Sam Shannon

Butterflies

In room 108, we are studying butterflies. One of the projects we are going make is butterfly art. We are going to make a picture out of the wings. Sometimes we get to go out two at a time and catch butterflies. Then we come in and look it up, write down the name in a journal, and let it go. We bring butterfly wings from home. I think butterfly research has been very fun. One of our goals is to catch a Monarch Butterfly. We also have a whole table of butterflies that we can look at under a microscope. It is very interesting to look at a butterfly up close.

By Vicki Albright

HOLA!

This means hello in Spanish. We are here to teach you some Spanish and play a word game.
Our Spanish center has books. Lots of people come to this center to read the books that are here. Everyday our teacher puts some Spanish on our schedule. At the end of the day, she reads it to us.

By Ashley McClain
Kelly Smith

The following words are Spanish. You need to find out what they mean in English and circle the English word on the puzzle.
GOOD LUCK!

1. pescado
2. pulpo
3. tucan
4. oceano
5. culebra
6. relampago
7. cofre del tesoro
8. caballito de mar
9. delfin
10. dosel

```
T R E A S U R E C H E S
L S A S E T E R C H N O K
K E L I G H T E N I N G K
Z A R Z D B L I G H Z R N
N A G F I S H D I S N A K
Q O M Z H R S C U G H O R
J R A V D D L P H I N Z M
K S T N H M O Z O S K M S
N E O R R T K R N S N Z Q
R E N O C A N Z T O U C A
E N R O Z K T H U N O C H
O Z C A N O P Y R C A O N
```

Management techniques are different for each individual facilitator. Empowered teachers usually adapt ideas and management suggestions to meet the needs and personalities of their group of learners. Each community of learners is unique in their interests and learning strategies. The classroom community develops its own distinctive personality as the year progresses. This requires a particularly flexible and highly personalized set of management techniques.

Chapter 11
In Conclusion

There is no real conclusion to theme study. The end of one study carries over into the next and surfaces as prior knowledge. Theme studies motivate the teacher as well as the students. As the students are searching for the answers to their theme study questions, the teacher is experiencing the same kind of curiosity about the student's learning. The classroom becomes one big research laboratory with the teacher as the head researcher.

Teacher Research

There are many different types of research that can be conducted in any classroom. The needs that arise in the classroom dictate the type of research required. The research itself can range from a simplistic form of observation to a complex form of gathering numerical statistics. It is important to research small concepts of learning as well as the large ones, because everything that happens in the classroom is significant. Conducting research helps us grow as professionals. We begin to recognize and understand the learners, which gives us the knowledge needed to provide a more meaningful, purposeful, and authentic curriculum.

Three years after I began implementing theme study into my curriculum, I began to wonder how children would feel if they were asked to research a topic that they truly had no interest in at all. I was certain that the topics were always broad enough that some point of interest could be found for every student. But what if the whole topic was of no interest? I wondered how a learner could cope. So I decided that as soon as our school year was over in May, I would begin to study some topic that I personally had no interest in whatsoever. I decided to study birds. Until this time in my life, birds were a part of nature that I knew existed but held no fascination for me.

School was out, and the deck surrounding my house seemed like the logical place to observe and learn about birds. As I took my place in a comfortable gliding chair, I inventoried my equipment. A poor pair of binoculars, a field guide from the public library, a pen, and a journal seemed to be the only tools needed. While I waited patiently for the first bird to fly my way, I petted one of our several cats who live outside. My home is surrounded by a wooded area only a few miles from the Mississippi River. The area should have been rich with rare and wonderful birds, but the first one to land in the yard was a robin. This was the one bird that I could recognize, and I was very disappointed that this was the only feathered species in sight. I'm not sure what I expected. Perhaps a toucan that had lost its way from the tropical rain forest would have been nice. As I hoped, the robin left and in flew an unrecognizable (to me) bird. I immediately raised my binoculars and noticed it was brown. Laying the binoculars aside, I thumbed through the field guide in search of a brown bird. To my surprise, there were at least ten pages of brown birds. I lifted the binoculars for a second look at the specimen in the yard. The field guide directed me to observe the beak as a point of reference. The beak was pointed, and as for length, I knew so little about birds that I couldn't judge short from long. I returned to the field guide which directed me to look at the tail of the bird. But, as was no surprise, when I looked for the unknown bird for the third time, it had flown away. In an early journal entry I wrote, "As a novice, it is hard to grasp all the identifying features in one glance." Children feel the same way. It is difficult to comprehend the enormous amount of information that they gather during research. They need time to read and make sense of the gathered information. Novice researchers will not be perfect researchers when they begin a study, but they will learn from their mistakes, and grow. The bird returned later, and I quickly checked for color, size, shape of tail, and beak. Because of my lack of observation knowledge, I had lost the first bird, but I learned to increase my observation skills to accomplish my goal. Goals are accomplished through both gathering knowledge and making connections.

After a month of bird-watching and a large number of log entries, my journal accounts and my behavior revealed that I had entered a new phase of learning. I had found it necessary to increase the quality and quantity of my equipment. I made sure that I was up at dawn sneaking quietly to the deck with my new essential equipment. I bought a spotting scope, a new pair of zoom binoculars, a song bird call, three field guides, art pencils, colored pencils, and an art gum eraser. All of these items were neatly tucked away in a basket for easy transporting. I was hooked!

Years have passed since I embarked on my research endeavor, and as I sit on my deck writing this chapter, my binoculars and field guide are only inches away. I have grown from an uninterested novice bird watcher into an avid bird watcher. Throughout my theme study teacher research, I have acquired valuable information about how children progress through different phases of the process. When I reread my journal entries, I am struck by my early statements of realization.

June 3   "I hear the birds singing in the woods, but I haven't a clue as to the bird behind the song. Inspired by the unknown, I drove to the library and checked out four albums of bird voices. This should correct my ignorance."

In this entry, I was reacting in the same way students do when they have unanswered questions. They decide what resource will answer their questions, and they collect the information that will satisfy their curiosity.

June 6   "Now a new twist comes into play. The birds, like people, do not look the same as juveniles as they do when they are mature adults. I guess I thought that all birds were adults. Identification has become more difficult. I'm generalizing knowledge into other areas. I'm reordering my thought patterns to take this new information into consideration for each new sighting. I no longer look only at the adult description. I now take into account that the birds could be immature which may give them a totally different color and size."

Children face new realizations every day all day long. Their minds are always reordering thoughts to accommodate their newly acquired information. This is a common occurrence for all students.

June 17   "It is so difficult to remember the individual voices of the birds when there is no familiar ground to establish a language connection. I can't remember the voices when I hear them. I need a technique to correct this problem."

Realizing a weakness exists and seeking a strategy to correct it, is what adults do. But children are usually at a loss as to what strategy would effectively correct their problem. That is why it is necessary to facilitate the students individually. Each of them will demonstrate a slightly different weakness and will need to be given special strategies to strengthen their abilities.

June 20   "The more you learn, the more you realize how little you know."

All students need to realize that learning is something we do all the time. We never stop learning, no matter how old we become.

This was a personal kind of research that helped me believe that regardless of the topic, there will always be some aspect of interest in a theme study that will satisfy each learner in the class. This will be true always, if we as facilitators are sensitive to the needs of the students. Theme study that is meaningful and authentic will always be accepted by the community of learners.

I have conducted classroom research in several of the subject areas in order to discover new strategies for those who struggle with different aspects of learning. In spelling, I found that reading increases the students' abilities more than any other strategy. I created a spelling assessment that fits my grade level and I administered it on a monthly basis. In order to monitor growth, a percentage was calculated for each child every month. I quickly became aware of the strategies needed to increase their abilities and presented those strategies through the writing process.

In math, I did an in-depth statistical piece of research for which the results showed that individualizing or grouping by each student's preferred learning style or strategy significantly increased the student's mathematical abilities. After discovering the individually preferred strategies, the students received one-on-one instruction. The results proved that this was an extremely effective method for teaching math.

In every type of research conducted, whether it is a systematic, statistical undertaking or a simple observation, the underlying purpose is to understand better the learners in your classroom. The research results will reveal the need for strategies that will strengthen their weak areas and enhance their strong areas. We conduct research in our classrooms for the sole purpose of providing a more informed kind of instruction within the curriculum.

There is one major key to implementing research results. The key is to be what you want your students to be. *No matter* what your conclusions are to any given problem, the students will take the new strategies seriously only if you do. The old adage, "Practice what you preach," is extremely relevant when it applies to the teacher/student relationship. Teachers have to model all that they teach, whether it is a skill, strategy, or even a behavior. A perfect example of this occurred during our study of endangered animals. The theme study led us naturally into a discussion of disappearing habitats. As a result of the brainstorming session, a learning center called Problems and Solutions was set up. In the center were books on various forms of pollution, pesticides, illegal poaching, rain forest destruction, etc. The children went to the center to decide what problem was the cause of their chosen animal's endangerment. Once they found the causes, they would draw their own conclusions and determine what would be the best solution to their problems.

At an early morning class meeting, one of the students expressed a concern about the plight of the spotted owl. She suggested

that we could save trees if we took our own bags to the store when we shopped. I enthusiastically commented on how this child had worked through her animal's problem and had formulated a simple and practical solution. I encouraged the students to think of ways to follow through with this forest-saving idea. They thought of everything, from not using any bags to carrying reusable cloth bags. Then came the precious "Let's see if Mrs. Strube really means what she says," question. In front of the whole class, one of the students asked me point blank if I intended to carry a reusable bag now that I knew that it would help save the spotted owl. Children call us to task. They search to find out if we are indeed going to "practice what we preach," or if it is just "an act" that we perform daily. That night I found myself driving to the local All-in-One Mart, purchasing a reusable red net bag, shopping, and trying to explain to the checkout clerk that I wanted to use my new bag in place of the paper bags they offered. The clerk's reply was, "You want to use it *now*?" I walked out with everything in my reusable bag except the 50-pound bag of dog food. I took my bag to school the next day as if it were my "show and tell" item.

I still continue to use my bag today. It gives me a good feeling every time I use it. Not because I'm saving the environment single-handedly, but because my students know that what I preach or teach, I also practice. In this same way, I share my interest and enthusiasm about the theme study. What we believe is important will be a top priority for the children as well.

Bibliography:

Altwerger, B., & B. Flores.
"The Theme Cycle: An Overview." In The Whole Language Catalog.
Santa Rosa, CA: American School Publishers, Macmillan/McGraw-Hill, 1991.

Bruner, J. S.
Toward a Theory of Instruction.
Cambridge, MA: The Belknap Press of Harvard University Press, 1966.

Goodman, K.
What's Whole in Whole Language?
New York: Scholastic, Inc., 1986.

Graves, D. H.
Writing: Teachers and Children at Work.
Exeter, NH: Heinemann Educational Books,1983.

Harste, J. C.; K. G. Short & C. Burke.
Creating Classrooms for Authors: The Reading-Writing Connection.
Portsmouth, NH: Heinemann, 1988.

Peterson, R. L. & M. Eeds.
Grand Conversations.
New York: Scholastic, Inc., 1990.

Smith, F.
Writing and the Writer.
New York: CBS College Publishing, 1982.

Appendix

Theme Study Resource Inventory

Sign-Up Sheet for Theme Centers

Oral Report Evaluation

Final Draft Writing Evaluation

Daily Schedules

Parent Report Form

THEME STUDY RESOURCE INVENTORY

PRINT RESOURCES

	Type	Title	Call Number
1.			
2.			
3.			
4.			
5.			
6.			
7.			
8.			
9.			
10.			
11.			
12.			
13.			
14.			
15.			
16.			
17.			
18.			
19.			
20.			

NON-PRINT RESOURCES

	Type	Title	Call Number
1.			
2.			
3.			
4.			
5.			
6.			
7.			
8.			
9.			
10.			

HUMAN RESOURCES

	Trade	Name	Address & Phone No.
1.			
2.			
3.			
4.			
5.			

SIGN-UP SHEET FOR THEME CENTERS

TIME	Mon.	Tue.	Wed.	Thur.	Fri.
8:45-9:00					
9:15-9:30					
10:30-10:45					
10:45-11:00					
11:00-11:15					
11:15-11:30					
11:30-11:45					
11:45-12:00					
12:30-12:45					
12:45-1:00					
1:00-1:15					
1:15-1:30					
1:30-1:45					
1:45-2:00					
2:30-2:45					
2:45-3:00					

ORAL REPORT EVALUATION

Student's Name _____

Date _____

Subject _____

Report Evaluation

5   Always

4   Usually

3   Sometimes

2   Seldom

1   Never

❑ Report was introduced with a title.

❑ Report was given in student's own language.

❑ Student spoke loudly.

❑ Student spoke clearly.

❑ Student gave report without looking at notes.

❑ Student had good knowledge of subject.

❑ Student included a visual aid with report.

❑ Student could answer questions presented by the audience.

❑ Student took the oral report seriously.

FINAL DRAFT WRITING EVALUATION

Name: _____

Date: _____

Kind of Writing: _____

MECHANICS

Capitalization: Beginning sentences ❏   ____ ____ ____
                     Titles ❏
                     Proper nouns ❏

Punctuation: End marks .❏ ?❏ !❏   ____ ____ ____

Commas: In a series ❏   ____ ____ ____
                     Direct address ❏
                     Yes and no ❏
                     Dates ❏
                     Between clauses of compound sentences ❏

Quotations: Quotation marks ❏   ____ ____ ____
                     Indent ❏
                     Commas ❏
                     End punctuation ❏

PARTS OF SPEECH

Nouns: Plurals ❏   ____ ____ ____
                     Possessive: Singular ❏   Plural ❏

Pronouns: Used as subjects ❏   ____ ____ ____
                     Possessive ❏
                     Usage of I and Me ❏

Verbs: Linking ❏   ____ ____ ____
                     Tense: Present ❏   Past ❏   Future ❏
                     Usage: ❏

Adjectives: Positive ❏   Comparative ❏   Superlative ❏   ____ ____ ____

Adverbs: Modifies a verb ❏   Modifies an adjective ❏   ____ ____ ____

Contractions: (   )   ____ ____ ____

Homophones: (   )   ____ ____ ____

SENTENCE STRUCTURE

Sentence clarity: Run-on ❏   Simple ❏   Expanded ❏   ____ ____ ____
                     Compound ❏   Variety ❏

Subject and verb agreement: ____ ____ ____

Written Expression: Content   ____ ____ ____

Spelling: ____ ____

Penmanship: Cursive ❏   Manuscript ❏   ____

DAILY SCHEDULES

DATE: _____

LEADERS: _____

STORY STATUS

Day #1 Rehearsal _____

Day #2 Pre-writing _____

Day #3 Rough Draft _____

Day #4 Self-Revision _____

Day #5 Team Revision _____

Day #6 Self-Edit _____

Day #7 Peer Edit _____

Day #8 Conference _____

Day #9 Corrections _____

Day #10   Final Draft _____

8:30-8:45   SSR

8:45-9:00   CLASS MEETING

9:00-9:30   LANGUAGE ARTS

1.

2.

3.

4.

9:30-10:30   **ART**

10:30-11:30   **MATH:**   PG __-__;   (EX __-__)   (WB__)

11:30-11:50   **ORAL READING:** _____

12:25-12:30   LUNCH

12:25-12:30   REST ROOM

12:30-2:00   **LANGUAGE ARTS**   1.

2.

3.

4.

5.

2:00-2:20   RECESS

2:20-3:00   **SCIENCE/SOCIAL STUDIES:**   1.

2.

3.

4.

5.

3:00-3:10   **JOURNAL**

3:10-3:15   CLASSROOM JOBS

....

HOME ASSIGNMENTS: 1.

2.

3.

133

PARENT REPORT FORM

Dear Parents,

    I will be keeping much of your child's work at school in his/her personal portfolio. If at any time your child's grades fall below average, I will contact you immediately.

    These grades reflect the progress of your child in recent days. Please look over the attached papers and ask your child about the assignments. The work that generated the grades written in the boxes is stapled to this sheet. Grades that appear in parentheses were generated by work that is either in a spiral notebook, or portfolio, or it has been made into a booklet. You are welcome to view these papers at any time. All of the saved work will be sent home at the end of the school year. If you have any questions concerning your child's work, use the back of the grade sheet for comments and give it to your child to return to me. I will respond to your questions as soon as possible.

Sincerely,

Mrs. Strube

PLEASE CUT ALONG DOTTED LINE AND RETURN

MATH _____

ENGLISH _____   SEE ATTACHED PAGE

SPELLING _____ ❏ ❏ ❏ ❏ ❏

CURSIVE _____ ❏ ❏ ❏ ❏ ❏

SOCIAL STUDIES: THEME (_____)
         _____ ❏   _____ ❏   _____ ❏
         _____ ❏   _____ ❏   _____ ❏
         _____ ❏   _____ ❏   _____ ❏

SCIENCE: THEME (_____)
         _____ ❏   _____ ❏   _____ ❏
         _____ ❏   _____ ❏   _____ ❏
         _____ ❏   _____ ❏   _____ ❏

READING   ❏ ❏ ❏ ❏ ❏ ❏

The / means your child failed to turn in the assignment.

Parent signature: _____

Notes

Notes